C000276933

To ANDREW CROSBY

DE,
UNDER Plumber, Painter, Glazier, Paper
REPAIRS.
110, EAST STREET,

EVERY DESCRIPT
tioners
GEORGE ELLIOTT,
...ultural Engineer, Brass Founder, Coppersmit
WHEELWRIGHT, &c.,
...REET, & 44, DOWNING STREET, FARNHAM
Agent for all kinds of Agricultural Implements.
...ERVATORIES AND OTHER BUILDINGS HEATED BY HOT WATER

THOMAS MATHEWS & CO,
BREWERS OF
...Ale, Stout, Porter and Pale Ale,
...RNH   WEST ST., BREWERY,   REY.
A.A.   R.A.C.   M.U.

JAMES PARRATT,
Builder and Undertaker,
3, BOROUGH,
FARNHAM.
Estimates given for all kinds of Repairs.

C. SMITHER,
...holsterer, Cabinet & Blind Maker,
...enter, Paperhanger & Decorator,
...R, DOWNING STREET,
FARNHAM.
...ED 1847.
SPECIALITY.
...ANNED AND L
...orders always
...IONS.   OUR GOODS
ARE SMART.
...your requirements?
FARNHAM.
CARRIAGE AND
BODY BUILDERS
MOTOR ENGINEERS
OUR PRICES
ARE KEEN.

HEATH & WILTSHIRE
LIMITED
FARNHAM, ALDERSHOT & BORDON.
ANY TYPE OF BODY BUILT
COMPETENT STAFF OF MECHANICS
FARNHAM
Tel. 188.
193

Delaunay Studio,
Farnham.

M
Eugene Fuller,   E. E. Simmonds.
Artist and Photographer.

Dairy-f
PORK
...e and Sn
...lies.
...N DAILY

"POST'S"
-Yeager and Man-O'War
FARNHAM.
SOLD ON THE MOST APPROVED PRINCIPLE

FARNHAM PAST

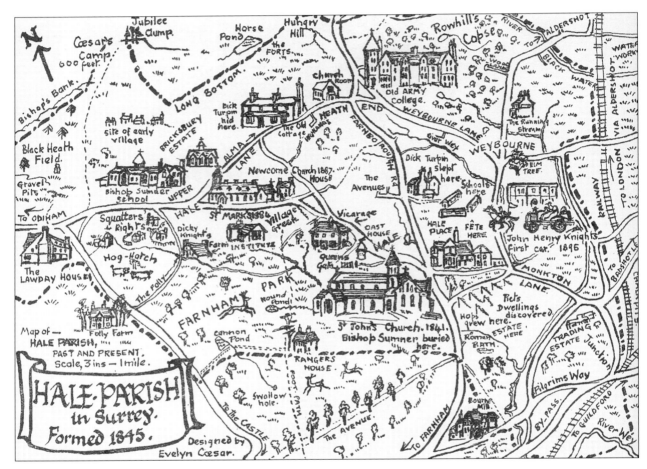

This map of Hale Parish, which was formed in 1845, was drawn by Evelyn Caesar, a former school teacher and grand-daughter of the first headmaster of the Bishop Sumner (later known as Hale) School.

FARNHAM
PAST

Jean Parratt

Phillimore

1999

Published by
PHILLIMORE & CO. LTD.
Shopwyke Manor Barn, Chichester, West Sussex

© Jean Parratt, 1999

ISBN 1 86077 105 X

Printed and bound in Great Britain by
BIDDLES LTD.
Guildford, Surrey

Contents

List of Illustrations

Frontispiece: Sketch map of Hale Parish, formed in 1845

Acknowledgements

The following people have been kind enough to lend me photographs and assist in a variety of ways in the preparation of this volume and I should like to thank each one for his or her enthusiastic help and interest and for giving me permission to use their words and/or pictures, as appropriate: Margaret Mullery, 36, 59, 61, 103; Peggy Chapman, 140, 148; Kath Riddles, 54, 58, 79; Wendy Hobart, 14, 26, 63, 76, 78, 94; Eddie Trusler, 92; Chris Shepheard, 5, 21, 47, 51, 62, 89, 135; Martin Rice, 6, 10, 93, 118, 119; Downing Street Studios, 75; Peter Towns, 49, 111, 116; Sheila Phillips, 20; Pam and John Hawkins, 145; Kerry Hawkins, 43; Jim Bodkin, 80, 81; Janet Booth, 108; Graham Collyer, 130, 131; David Rose, 130, 131; Doug Nye, 120, 121; Frank Pullinger, 12, 18, 71, 83; Lynn Hutchings, 8, 33, 112, 113, 123; Mike Leishman, 57; Diane Honan, 101; Audrey Wells, 143; William Serpant, 56; Gwen Graham, 17, 37, 38, 65, 104, 106, 107; Jonathan Durham, 88; Paul and Ian Fletcher, 28; the late Maurice Elphick, 115; Mark Parratt, 1; Gill Hollingworth, 31; The Cobbett Society, 60; Terence Blackwell, 68; Jean Thorpe, 98; Caryl Griffith (for photographs taken by the late Edward Griffith and reprinted by Martin Rice), Leni Grosset, Bernadine Collins, Chris Hellier, Dennis Stone, Andrew Lodge, Rosalind Crowe, Brian Howarth, Anne Jones, David and Stuart Roberts and Ted Parratt, my husband, for his help and for always being on hand when needed.

Farnham Past *is dedicated to all Farnham school teachers, past and present, but in particular to three to whom I owe a depth of gratitude—Denis Kelly (head at the former Park School, Hale Road, who first employed me in a school); the late Eddie Godsil (senior master at the former Farnham Grammar School, who instructed both my husband and son and told me many anecdotes about this town); and the late Betty Hair, who taught English to both my daughter and me, at the former Farnham Girls' Grammar School. Her presence has remained with me always and I feel her checking every word I write.*

One

Prehistoric Farnham

THE HISTORY OF FARNHAM goes back to the very early days of the river which we now call the Wey. From Wrecclesham in the west, to Snailslynch in the east, on the southern side of the river there are three gravel spreads or terraces which lie uniformly and about fifty feet apart. Each terrace is a relic bed of the Farnham river and the gravel contents of each deposit represents debris of old land surfaces. Their different heights indicate the changes in the elevation of the land surface. The depth of the river today, below the height of the land at Wrecclesham (the highest and therefore the oldest terrace), gives an indication of the antiquity of the area.

The debris in the gravel terraces includes stone tools such as palaeolithic hand axes. Similar tools have been found in France and in a number of other gravel valleys in this country. Archaeologists have studied these implements and have assigned them to several different, but successive, primitive cultures—Chellean, Acheulian and Mousterian—and each type occurs in Farnham. A road at The Bourne is named Acheulian Way because of the implements of this period which were discovered there when the houses were being constructed. The earliest nomads to make use of the gravel in this area, known as people of the Old Stone Age, are believed to have worked their flints here about 100,000 B.C.

Mammoth remains, including a splendid tusk on show at the Museum of Farnham, have been found on the lowest terrace of gravel, which extends from Wrecclesham to a spot close to the *Princess Royal* public house at Runfold, in the east. Gravel was once extracted from a pit at Weydon, now a grassed area behind houses in Upper Way, and at Snailslynch, close to the river and about one mile east from Farnham town centre. In the early 1930s a number of mammoth teeth, shells, and a piece of peat encased in redeposited clay, containing pollen grains of plants which were contemporary with the mammoth, were also found close to Snailslynch.

Throughout the entire length and on both sides of the river valley, through the area we now call Farnham, cultivation has exposed many items such as microliths, scrapers and flakes indicating later Stone Age inhabitants, and in the past, when there were many more fields than housing estates around the town, the farmer's plough turned up such vast quantities of flint tools as to indicate settlements. One such site, where a number of pit dwellings dug out as shelters by mesolithic people *c.*6,000 B.C. were found, was close to the present sewage treatment works in Monkton Lane and near to the Six Bells roundabout. When this site was excavated by archeologists in 1930, they found, for the first time in this country, a complete mesolithic flint industry. It included a very large number of flint pygmy implements which are very small but geometrically shaped and were described by one of the archeologists as being the most amazing products of any prehistoric culture. They also found bones of a sheep, a pig and a small animal rather like a species of ox. The finds were distributed, at that time, between the British Museum, Guildford Museum and the University Museum of Ethnology at Cambridge. A suitably inscribed stone marks this site, recorded by the archaeologist W.F. Rankine, as the 'Mesolithic Settlement which is the most important in the British Isles.'

To really appreciate why this place was so attractive to early man and woman, one should have a little knowledge of the geology of the area, which is simple but varied. There is sand, clay and chalk, with gravel overlays, and in a line which stretches roughly from West Street, through The Borough and out to the end of East Street is an extensive layer of the Lower Greensand, the oldest deposit in the district and dating from the Cretaceous period of about seventy million years ago. It extends to Hindhead and has layers of ironstone in it as well as, near Churt, bargate stone from which a number of local buildings have been constructed, including Dockenfield Church of the Good Shepherd. The vegetation on this sandy ground is rather sterile and usually only plants such as heather, gorse and pine grow well on it.

To the north of the West Street/East Street line is a belt of clay which varies in width. This is the Gault Clay which was used by Roman potters in the area and, more recently, by the Harris family at Wrecclesham Potteries. Numerous fossils of sea creatures have been found in the clay, including sharks' teeth which were found by Jim Nixon, one of the pottery workers, in the 1930s.

1   A marker similar to a gravestone, and incised by a mason at H.C. Patrick, marks the site of the first village in this country at the Shepherd and Flock (formerly Tin Hut) roundabout. Professor Rankine, headmaster of Badshot Lea School, helped in the excavation work in the 1930s.

2   Absolem Harris founded Wrecclesham Pottery in 1872. Here he examines one of the owl jugs for which the firm was famed. Born in 1837, Absolem opened his first pottery, at Elstead, in 1860. He married a Miss Freemantle and they had six children. He was still working in 1928, the year of his death. A rare, brick-built bottle kiln at Wrecclesham is currently under restoration.

North of the Gault Clay is a belt of chalk-like rock known as Upper Greensand, although it is not sand at all, and above this is chalk. This can easily be seen by anyone who walks in Farnham Park along the ridge known as The Avenue, or those who walk behind the Surrey Institute of Art and Design University College and up to the path behind Three Stiles Road, to an area known earlier this century as Rawley's Ridge. Farnham Castle is also built on the chalk ridge. To the west of the town the chalk opens up into the Hampshire farming area and to the east it rises into the stretch now known as the Hog's Back.

North of the chalk there is a layer of clay, known as Reading Clay, and over this lies a deposit of London Clay, used in the past for local brickmaking. This clay also contains fossils and sharks' teeth, which could suggest the climate here was sub-tropical at the time the clay was deposited. Above the London Clay comes what is known as the Bagshot Sands. Hale is particularly noted for this, although gravel hides a lot of the sand.

The range of geological deposits here has meant that industries have grown up around them, such as the potteries, brickfields, gravel extraction for the building trade, and stone quarrying for building walls and houses. In prehistoric times the chalk, which has rich layers of flint nodules, attracted Stone Age men who made their implements from the flint. In addition, the plentiful supply of water attracted game. There was food and drink as well as materials for tools; what more could early man have wanted?

For about three hundred years, c.2500-2200 B.C., people living in what has become known as the neolithic period inhabited this area. They made pottery, polished flint tools, chipped flint axes and leaf-shaped arrowheads, and hunted. In 1935 W.F. Rankine found the remains of a neolithic long barrow (a burial mound) in the chalk at Badshot Lea. The centre of the mound had been removed during chalk quarrying but most of its contents were still intact, including some pottery. In addition great quantities of bones, including those of red deer, ox, pig and sheep, were found. This was the first long barrow to have been discovered in Surrey but now it has completely disappeared under a housing development.

The neolithic period was followed by the Bronze Age (c.1800-750 B.C.), and within a half-mile of the site of the mesolithic pit dwellings and the neolithic long barrow, a Bronze-Age burial urn, filled with fragments of cremated bones, was found earlier this century, beneath a cairn of chalk boulders. Other smaller Bronze-Age urns have been found to the south-west of Farnham, including some at Green Lane, which was an urn-field or burial ground and which still has a graveyard there to the present day. Flint tools were still being made and used at this time and a number of them have been found in the Tilford district.

Flint tools were still in use in the Iron Age (c.500-75 B.C.). Pottery of this period, as well as crudely made flint implements, have been found at Caesar's Camp, a typical Iron-Age site which is north of the town on the Hampshire/Surrey border, near Hale. Other smaller Iron-Age earthworks and cattle enclosures have been located at The Sands, near the *Barley Mow* public house and at Botany Hill, Crooksbury.

The Iron Age is really the beginning of more recent historical times. The area we now call Farnham must have continued to be attractive as a place to live—even to those who had come from warmer climes like Italy—because the Romans built both a bath and villa within 200 yards of the mesolithic settlement of 6000 B.C., less than half-a-mile from where both neolithic and Bronze-Age burials took place, and within two miles of Caesar's Camp to the north and The Sands to the south-east, where Iron-Age settlers kept their cattle.

To quote W.F. Rankine again, in his writings about Farnham: 'There may be regions where any one of these prehistoric phases is more richly represented, but there are few, if any, where such a coherent succession may be followed.'

Two

Veni, Vidi, Vici …

FOR AT LEAST TWO HUNDRED years after *Britannia Romana*, by Horsley, was published in 1732, it was believed that Farnham was the site of the Roman town of Vindomis. Although it is now possible to refute this statement, Farnham was nevertheless an important place during the Roman occupation of this country from A.D. 43–410 and the remains of several potteries and kilns have been found.

In addition a villa and bath were discovered a mile east of the present town centre during building works in 1946-7.

The first floor of the first pair of houses to be built had been completed and the ground was being dug for the next pair when a workman, Robert Chadwick, noticed a floor which was later found to be part of a Roman bath. Work was stopped on the first pair of houses,

3 The head of Emperor Lucius Septimus Severus, whose period of office extended from A.D. 193-211, was found on the only three coins ever recovered at the site of the Roman villa in Farnham. He was born in Leptis Magna, near the modern city of Homs, Libya, on 11 April 146 and died in England, at York, on 4 February 211.

4 On 27 January 1998, Bessie Bramley, left, and her sister, Mary Siegnot, were present at an informal ceremony to unveil a plaque on a house in Roman Way, Farnham. It marks the site of remains of a Roman villa and bath which were discovered by their late father, Robert Chadwick, a workman at the site, in 1946.

5   Much evidence of Roman pottery kilns, from the first to fourth centuries, can be found in Farnham, including these remains which were excavated in Farnham Park close to the swallow-hole used to feed water to the Roman bath and villa about 400 yards away, in the present Roman Way.

and a request was made to the Ministry of Works for permission to pull down that part of the building which had been constructed. With building bricks being scarce so soon after the end of the Second World War, permission was refused and the building continued upwards, although both the bath site and the part of the villa which had not been built upon were excavated. The archaeologists were assisted by German prisoners-of-war, who lived in a large house at Tongham, before they were repatriated to their own country. On 27 January 1998 a plaque was unveiled on a house in Roman Way by the two daughters of Robert Chadwick, Bessie and Mary, to mark the site of the bath and villa for posterity.

Archaeologists involved with the excavation work at this place, originally called the Six Bells estate but later renamed Roman Way, decided that the bath must have been used by pottery workers and that the water for it had

been brought by aqueduct from what is now Farnham Park. In the late 1960s, when William Old, a firm of contractors, was building a road to join the former Tin Hut roundabout (now known as the Six Bells roundabout) to the Shepherd and Flock roundabout, they were unable to stop water flowing on to the new road, despite pumps being used day and night. Eventually it was realised that the aqueduct was still functioning, and so a culvert was constructed to channel the water into a nearby stream close to Bourne Mill, one of the Farnham mills mentioned in Domesday Book.

Whatever the Roman skills at road building, it was not necessary for them to build a new one through the place now known as Farnham. A prehistoric trackway, subsequently to be known as the Harrow Way, crossed the area. This had probably come into existence during either the Bronze Age or early Iron

6 Bourne Mill in the 1960s, taken by Edward Griffith, photographer and model railway enthusiast. There was a waterfall to the rear of the building, only the occasional car passed by and the present site of today's greenhouses and conservatories was a pleasant garden where afternoon tea, bought from the building which then sold antiques, could be enjoyed in the summer months.

7 The avenue of trees leading to Farnham Castle along the ridge from the park's eastern boundary. It is believed to have been part of an Iron-Age road. The park was once full of deer, the property of whichever Bishop held the See. This was where Henry VIII and other monarchs rode when staying at the castle.

The Weekly Telegraph, November 10, 1934.

Princess Marina At Home

The WEEKLY TELEGRAPH

The MOST INTERESTING JOURNAL in the WORLD

No. 3786   Family Insurance   1862   SEVENTY-THIRD YEAR OF PUBLICATION   1934   November 10, 1934   2D.

Registered as a newspaper and for transmission to Canada

THE ROADSIDE BARBER

8 In 1934 the *Weekly Telegraph* featured Alf Hutchings cutting Dick Ruffle's hair, at his open-air barber's beside the Tin Hut (later the Six Bells) roundabout, on its front page.

9 Despite the fact that the railway to London runs along the ridge on the left, this early 20th-century view of the oasthouses reflected in the River Wey at Snailslynch is a picture of perfect peace. Later, the oasts were converted into T.S. Swiftsure's headquarters, before a purpose-built unit was constructed for the cadets, at Badshot Lea.

Age, and continued to be used throughout the Roman and later periods. Many people believe that The Avenue in Farnham Park is part of this Iron-Age road.

Throughout the Roman occupation of this area the pottery industry thrived. Remains of kilns have been found at a number of sites including Farnham Park, the sewage treatment works in Monkton Lane, at Snailslynch, Stoneyfields and Green Lane, as well as over the Hampshire border into the Alice Holt Forest (part of which is now called Alice Holt Woodland Park). The pottery industry began in a small way but by the time of the Emperors Hadrian and Antoninus (in the second and third centuries A.D.) it was a much larger concern. During the latter part of the third century it is believed that the industry declined

and the bath at the Roman Way site deteriorated. It was then rebuilt and extensively buttressed to provide bathing facilities for the potters during the fourth century, the greatest time for Roman pottery manufacture in this area.

It is claimed by A.W.G. Lowther, an archaeologist concerned with the Six Bells site excavations, that the villa was for the use of a person in charge of the local potteries, and as his home it had its own suite of rooms devoted to bathing, including undressing, warm, hot and sweating rooms as well as a water 'plunge' bath, a large living room, and a staircase which led to two, or possibly three, rooms on the first floor. Most of the items made by the Romans in this area consisted of bowls, dishes and cooking pots of grey and black ware, and even today, almost 1,600 years since the Romans left the site, pieces of floor and heating tiles, as well as shards of pottery, still come to the surface after rain.

The Romans were succeeded by the Saxons, who gave Farnham its name. They gradually spread across this country, destroying Roman villas and disrupting means of communication by isolating towns, and although it is not known exactly when the Romans left Farnham it was probably at the beginning of the fifth century. However, the indigenous inhabitants, many of whom had learned the pottery trade from their Roman masters, remained and when the Saxons arrived they probably found a small but flourishing community where farming and pottery were the chief occupations.

Although Farnham is only about thirty miles from the south coast it was not occupied by the West Saxons but by those who came from the south kingdom of the Middle Saxons (Middlesex), who crossed the Thames before settling on its south bank and on the North Downs. Some of them moved still farther south and set up small communities throughout the area we now call Surrey—*Suthrige*, the south kingdom. Farnham was as far as these people went because here they encountered the dense Hampshire forests, which were a deterrent to

further progress. It is for this reason that the Farnham area of Surrey 'bulges' into Hampshire and why there are so many places, such as Rowledge, Heath End and Hale, where the county boundary separates houses on both sides of the same street. At Rowledge the boundary is said to go through the centre of the *Cherry Tree* public house.

The Saxons, like their predecessors, found this last-occupied place before the forests had an excellent water supply, a number of verdant water meadows where plenty of fern and bracken grew, and plenty of wood for building and burning. It was therefore an hospitable place; they named it *Fearnhamme*, and by this name it is called in the *Anglo-Saxon Chronicle*.

The Saxons are also given credit for the first Christian church in Farnham, which in all probability was at approximately the spot where St Andrew's Church is today. To date, the only early Saxon remains recorded in Farnham are those on high ground just behind the *William Cobbett* public house. The present homes on that site are in a thoroughfare known as Saxon Croft to commemorate the group of weavers' huts which once stood at the same spot. When gravel digging was taking place in 1924, the remains of one of the weaver's huts was exposed, together with a few clay loom weights, an iron knife blade,

10 Much of Farnham's wealth comes from wool. Here a student at Farnham School of Art, West Street, is sorting through the wool from a sheep, before spinning and, later, weaving the fibre, an occupation that has scarcely changed over hundreds of years. Saxon weaver's huts were found behind the *William Cobbett* at a place now known as Saxon Croft.

11 The tower of Farnham parish church looked like this until 1866, when it was raised to its present height. A plaque inside is dedicated to Andrew Windsor who died in 1620. In 1783 Catherine Eyre gave £50 to buy a new communion cloth and ornaments for the church, and in 1751 a Mr. Avenell was paid 10s. 6d. for a new dial to the clock.

a bronze clasp, a blue and yellow bead and some fragments of smooth brown pots. All the artefacts were dated to the sixth and seventh centuries.

By the middle of the seventh century Farnham had become a place of some worth and was then under the domination of the West Saxons, who had eventually pressed through the Hampshire forests and conquered this outpost of the south kingdom of the Middle Saxons.

At about this time Bishop Wilfrid, late of Lindisfarne and York, had been banished from the latter town and had taken refuge in the vast forest of Andreasweald, in Sussex, where he met the Saxon Prince, Caedwalla, who was also in exile. Wilfrid showed great kindness to the prince and converted him to Christianity.

Farnham became the property of the Church in A.D. 688 when Caedwalla, by then king, who had seized the Kingdom of the West Saxons, returned Wilfrid's kindness by making grants of land, including Farnham, to the Christian Church via Swithun, Bishop of Winchester. By this gift Caedwalla hoped he would appear better in the eyes of God. In the

British Museum there is a 12th-century copy of the charter from A.D. 688. In it Caedwalla states that he does

> ... confer on you in possession to build a monastery the land named Fernham in hides sixty ... with all things pertaining to them, fields, woods, meadows, pastures, fisheries, rivers, fountains; have ye from me free licence of giving or changing and in your will be it placed ... Done in the place called Basingshearh [Basing] in the year 688.

In *Between Four Bridges—A History of Badshot Lea* by Maurice Hewins, published in 1979, the author pinpoints, with the aid of *Saxon Farnham* by Mrs. W.O. Manning, part of the area of the land which Caedwalla gave to Farnham: '... [it] runs out onto the Heathfield [Blackheath field towards Caesar's Camp]—so to the oak swine pasture [Ash Dene?]—thence to the place of the shining water.' (In Saxon this was *Gloran Ige* and the place-name survived for over 1,100 years in the field name Glorney Mead, later corrupted to Lawney Meadow. It is now, rather appropriately, part of the Angling Society's flooded gravel pit off Weybourne Lane.) From here the Saxon boundaries continue 'to the middle of the swinewood (near Inwoods)—so to Seven Dykes' (banks on the Hog's Back above Shoelands). The land within these boundaries became the Manor of Farnham, and by A.D. 803 was in the hands of the Bishop of Winchester. In A.D. 976 King Edgar confirmed a gift of land across the Blackwater and set out the bounds of the Manor of Crondall, of which Aldershot became a Tithing. The name of Glorney Mead has now been used again, in a cul-de-sac, part of a housing development off Lower Weybourne Lane which was built in the early 1980s.

No Saxon monastery has ever been recorded as being built here but a church was constructed and, as has already been said, was in all probability where St Andrew's Church is still—on a raised mound to prevent flooding when the River Wey broke its banks. Saxon names can still be seen in the streets of Farnham: Dogflud and Gostrey both originate from about the eighth century A.D.

Crondall was also a manor of the Bishop of Winchester and both Farnham and Crondall were represented at the Bishop's Court, held on Blackheath Field. The area is still recorded

12 This drawing by Gordon Home, made in the first decade of the 20th century, shows one of the medieval parts of Farnham Castle, now the refectory.

by the word 'Lawday', which appears in both house and street names at Hale.

The boundaries laid down by Caedwalla were maintained for centuries by vigilance and resorting to law where necessary. Then the custom of beating the bounds was introduced. Originally boys were bumped, or beaten, at strategic boundary marks, so that they would remember them, should the need ever arise for the lads to be witnesses over a land dispute. This ceremony—without the physical violence—is still carried out today, by the priest and parishioners of Rowledge, to mark the village boundaries, although it is only to uphold a tradition. Accurate mapping now means that such ceremonies are unnecessary for legal purposes.

After the Saxons came the Danes, in the ninth century, and a battle took place in Fearnhamme in A.D. 893, when King Alfred's son, Edward the Elder, is said to have turned back part of the Danish army from here. The incident is believed to have taken place at either Charles Hill, Tilford, or Gong Hill, on the way to Frensham. A story which has been handed down for generations concerns the women of Farnham, who are said to have defended the town from a small band of the Danish enemy, from a vantage point in the earlier tower of the church of St Andrew, until their victorious menfolk returned from their battle with the invaders.

At this time Winchester was the capital of England, although London was already a very important place. Important people travelling between these towns would almost certainly have journeyed through Farnham. Therefore, it would seem that from the ninth century onwards the inhabitants would see kings such as Harold, Ethelred and Alfred passing by, and after Bishop Henry de Blois, brother of King Stephen, organised the building of Farnham Castle in 1147, these important personages would often have stayed in the town as well. The original fortress had a large hall, chapel, kitchen, domestic accommodation and a fortified keep. It was built of 'clunch' (white chalk stone) and must have looked very imposing to the townspeople who lived lower down the hill in the borough, which was enclosed by a ditch and a fence.

The townsfolk who lived within the borough were tradesmen, such as bakers and alehouse keepers, who had to pay money (a form of tax) to the Bishop of Winchester. But they did not have to work for him. Those people who lived in West Street, the lanes near the church, and farther afield had to work for the Lord of the Manor (the Bishop of Winchester) on his land as well as repair the castle, shear his sheep and collect wood for his fires—without pay.

Three

Priests and Place-names

A T THE TIME of the Norman Conquest, in 1066, Farnham was a small community of peasants who worked on the land. To the east of the town was, and still is, Bourne Mill, one of the few local places mentioned in Domesday Book of 1086. This mill is within 400 yards of both the mesolithic 'village' and the Roman bath and villa.

There were four men in Farnham who were important enough to be mentioned by name in Domesday Book. They were the priest, Osborn de Eu, Ralph, William and Wace. On the Bishop's land there were 36 villagers and 11 smallholders with 29 ploughs and 11 slaves. Between them Ralph, William and Wace held land on which there were 22 villagers and nine smallholders.

Each spring and autumn the Seneschal, an official from the Bishop of Winchester, held a court at Blackheath Field, a place which is marked today by the traffic lights controlling the vehicles coming north from Farnham town centre to the Folly Hill/Odiham Road junction. Here they meet the traffic coming from Hale and both then join the road to Odiham and Basingstoke. Names such as Lawday Lane, Lawday Link, Lawday Place and Lawday House are all indicators of the area to which people from not only the Farnham Hundred but also from as far afield as Cove and Farnborough had to come to pay their rent to the Bishop, in forms as diverse as pigs, horseshoes and honey.

The Seneschal also settled disputes, punished misdemeanours and ordered fines to be paid, as well as dealing with taxes which

were due on changes in land possession or on the marriages of daughters. In *The Story of Farnham*, Mrs. W.E. Newnam, a former resident of Castle Street, relates, 'On one occasion 100s. (£5) fine was paid by the whole "ville of Farnham" because of the escape of a certain robber.' Criminal cases were taken to Guildford to be judged by the King's Justices, though hangings took place both in Farnham and in the surrounding areas. Until relatively recently an area in Badshot Lea was still known as Gallows Field.

Under the Normans, the people of Farnham had to work hard for little recompense, though life for the town's inhabitants must have been better than for people who lived in country areas. Much more is known about Farnham's history than is known about many other places because the Bishop of Winchester kept very good records and accounts, and the *Winchester Pipe Rolls* give details of the receipts and expenditure in all his manors. From these Pipe Rolls scholars can determine how much was paid to people who worked for the Bishop, how much was spent and on which items of food by visitors staying at Farnham Castle, plus many other interesting facts.

Nineteen years before work started on building Farnham Castle monks began constructing a monastery at Waverley, the first Cistercian monastery in this country. The foundation stone was laid by William Giffard, who was the second Bishop of Winchester after the Norman Conquest.

13 John Rocque's map of Farnham, *c.*1768. Spellings of place-names have changed over two centuries: Heal (Hale), Weyburn (Weybourne), The Bone (The Bourne), Wrackles-ham (Wrecclesham), Bone Mill (Bourne Mill) and Lady House (Lawday House). Most of the main roads are easily identi-fiable including the route to Odiham, down Jockey (Jackal's) Hill. Rocque was a highly skilled, immigrant Huguenot surveyor.

14 On 24 November 1128, William Giffard, Bishop of Winchester, founded Waverley Abbey and brought 13 monks from the Cistercian house at Cisteaux, in Burgundy, to live in England at a location suited to the Cistercian ruling as being '... in a place remote from the conversation of men'. Women were rigidly excluded. The ruins are seen here in 1945.

15 It is difficult to imagine how masons such as these, with their simple tools, could have built such a magnificent edifice as Farnham Castle. In the 1930 production of the Rev. Neville Lovett's *Farnham Pageant*, Messrs. P.C. Carter, P. German, W.H. Hester, F. King, F.W. Lee, E. Lowe, H. Webber and W.C. Wiltshire played the masons' roles.

William Giffard was chancellor to King Henry I, and when he laid the stone on 24 November 1128 it was intended that the abbey should be for one abbot and 12 monks. When it was first completed the complex covered eight acres of land. In the original layout, which was completed in A.D. 1201, there was a large church, the abbot's house, a brewhouse, a guest house for important people such as members of the royal family, and accommodation for everyday travellers as well as the monks and lay brothers. Soon, however, the monks became noted for their agriculture, architecture and commerce, and they chose to commit more of the land they already owned to agriculture until it extended to over 500 acres, covering Wanborough,

Tongham and Aldershot. They established farms or granges on these outlying estates. In the 12th century the monks were forced to raise the monastery floors by two feet because of frequent flooding from the nearby River Wey. Waverley became one of the largest monastic foundations in England, supporting 70 monks and 120 lay brothers.

The first documentary evidence of monks from Waverley Abbey being in Aldershot is in the 1287 schedule of the Crondall Rental: 'Aldershot. The Monks of Waverley hold 31 acres of encroachment on payment of 4s. 3d. at the Feast of St Michael.' The site of this grange was close to St Michael's Church, in Church Lane East, and the acres farmed extended as far as the present Eggars Hill down to Boxall's Lane. The grange was manned by one monk and eight clerics, who between them tended many hundreds of sheep.

In the 13th century the borough was the same place designated as The Borough today, and stretched from the top of Downing Street to Bear Lane. There were also houses to the north of it stretching about halfway up Castle Street, and a similar area to the south. The parish church of St Andrew and the cluster of cottages around it was not within the borough confines.

About twenty-five years ago, when a building in Middle Church Lane was burnt to the ground, archaeologists found the remains of much earlier buildings beneath it, possibly the medieval homes of families who lived there more than six centuries earlier. Most people spent their time, then, trying to grow enough food to live on. They would cultivate small plots of vegetables, keep both bees, for their wax and honey, and hens for eggs as well as the occasional meal. There had long been millers: the *Winchester Pipe Rolls* show that in the Wey valley, near Farnham, were La Medmulle, La Burne, Highe Mill, Wulley Mill, Elstead Mill and Waverley Mill.

At about this time, some men were beginning to specialise in crafts and in buying and selling, especially items such as the wool from sheep, a necessity for clothing, and gradually the market at the bottom of Castle Street grew. At first, corn grown in fields away from the town, and wool, which had been shorn from sheep in the surrounding neighbourhood, would be sold. Later, when weavers started making woollen cloth, this too would be traded as well as fish (from the River Wey), animals, cheese, eggs and animal skins. In A.D. 1249 the Bishop of Winchester gave the people

16 Waverley Abbey House, from an old glass plate negative photographed about 1860. It was often visited by Florence Nightingale and was one of the large houses in this area used as a hospital in the First World War.

17 This is not a country lane; it is a thoroughfare in Farnham town centre, Vicarage Lane facing the parish church. The building behind the van was burned out in a fire and beneath it was evidence of medieval cottages. The site has since been developed. The white and black pointed roof unit was built in 1727 as Farnham's first workhouse.

18 Weydon Mill, one of the mills mentioned in Domesday Book, drawn in the 1930s by an artist with the initials A.G.E. All that remains at this point today is a bridge across the River Wey and a private house.

of Farnham a charter which allowed them to look after the market themselves in return for money which had to be paid to the Bishop. Part of the Town Charter, which is still in existence, reads:

> ... the said burgesses and their heirs for ever shall have all liberties and customs ... They shall have our Fair of Farnham at the feast of All Saints ... They shall yield to us twelve pounds of silver at Hock Day and at the Feast of St Martin ...

The original markets were held on Sunday, but after the time of King John the day was changed to Thursday. On fair days more people than usual came into town and, with amusements on hand as well as goods for sale, theft and cheating sometimes occurred. Such misdemeanours would be punished either by fines or a period in the stocks.

People from all over the Hundred would journey to Farnham on Sundays to attend church. Such attendance was not achieved without difficulty, especially in winter months, when journeys from Tyleford (Tilford), Twongham (Tongham), Badshate (Badshot Lea), Chert (Churt), Ronewyk (Runwick), Dupenhale

19   Five of Farnham's 'royal visitors', together on the castle lawns, in 1930. Left to right: Capt. Breton was King George III; Mr. Charles Morice was King Charles I; Miss J. Nicholson was Queen Elizabeth I; Mr. H. Webber was King Henry VIII, and Rev. Maj. J.E. Price was King John. They were all taking part in the *Farnham Pageant*.

(Dippenhall) and Wreclesham (Wrecclesham) must have been made along rough, muddy tracks and probably on foot. Those who lived within reach of Fernesham (Frensham), Elested (Elstead) and Sele (Seale) were more fortunate as there were chapels they could attend in those places. However, on special days in the church's calendar even these people would travel to the mother church and would there be joined by the people from Dogflude (East Street) and Westestrete (West Street), both of which were outside the borough boundary.

Church attendance was a diversion, a break from the hard, seemingly endless toil on the land. It was also a place where information could be exchanged, gossip related and people of the opposite sex other than family members could be encountered, an important matter for unmarried, peasant girls and young men. In the 14th century the Church forbade marriage between relations, it was not permitted to marry outside the manor, and a peasant was not allowed to marry someone who was free. Such restrictions made it very difficult to find a husband or wife, although things had been even more difficult before 1215. Until that time marriage was forbidden between all to the seventh degree, that is, to all those who had a common great-great-great-great-great-grandfather, but this, coupled with the other restrictions, meant that it was almost impossible for anyone to marry and the population had become static.

In *The Cost of Living in 1300*, Daphne Harper states that by A.D. 1300, in the area which stretched from the Hampshire border in the north to Hindhead in the south, and from Seale in the east to Bentley in the west, a total of about 1,400 people or 350 families eked out a living on what was, for much of the area, very poor land for growing crops. They were all tenants of the Bishop of Winchester and had to pay dues to him as well as support themselves. The death rate was only four per cent (56 per year), according to the statistics provided by Daphne Harper, but after the Black Death, the population of this area, and throughout the country, was reduced by between a quarter and one third, so that probably only about 1,000 men, women and children remained under the Bishop of Winchester, in his Manor of Farnham.

The following description, from *The Vision of Piers Plowman*, by William Langland (*c*.1332-1400), gives an example of the acute suffering and despair which our ancestors encountered in the everyday task of trying to stay alive.

As I went by the way, weeping for sorrow, I saw a poor man hanging on to the plough. His coat was of a coarse stuff which was called cary; his hood was full of holes and his hair stuck out of it. As he trod the soil his toes peered out of his worn shoes with their thick soles; his hose hung about his hocks on all sides and he was all bedaubed with mud as he followed the plough. He had two mittens, made scantily of rough stuff, with worn-out fingers and thick with muck. This man bemired himself in mud almost to the ankle, and drove four heifers before him that had become feeble, so that men might count their every rib as sorry-looking as they were.

His wife walked beside him with a long goad in a shortened cote-hardy looped up full high and wrapped in a winnowing-sheet to protect her from the weather. She went barefoot on the ice so that the blood flowed. And at the end of the row lay a little crumb-bowl, and therein a little child covered with rags, and two two-year-olds were on the other side, and they all sang one song that was pitiful to hear; they all cried the same cry—a miserable note. The poor man sighed sorely, and said 'children, be still.'

This is not a description of a Farnham family, but it could have applied to almost any peasant in this country in the second half of the 14th century, and a very good idea of how the year appeared to the peasants toiling on the land can be gleaned from a table of medieval names given to the months: January-Wintermonth; February-Mudmonth; March-

Springmonth; April-Eastermonth; May-Joymonth; June-Ploughmonth; July-Haymonth; August-Harvestmonth; September-Windmonth; October-Vintagemonth; November-Autumnmonth; December-Holymonth.

It is recorded that in 1300, when peasants still had to do the haymaking for the Bishop of Winchester as well as to collect huge amounts of firewood for the castle (without pay, needless to say), a group of men, from seven tithings, rebelled and went on strike. They were fined. Every man over 14 years had to be a member of a tithing and in Farnham they were Dogflud, Westestrete, Elested, Sele, Twongham, Wreclesham, Fernesham, Chert, Tyleford, Cunton, Badshate, Runvale, Runewyck, Dupenhale, Benetlyghe, Crundal and Waneburgh. Every peasant had to pay money, known as the tithing penny, at the twice-yearly courts held at Lawday House, at the top of Castle Hill, at Martinmas (11 November) and Hockaday (two weeks after Easter Tuesday).

The tithing penny was only one of a number of injustices meted out to peasants. Other examples were the fine that had to be paid to the Bishop by anyone who wished to leave Farnham, and even if sufficient money were available to pay the fine, permission to leave could be refused if the Bishop did not want to lose a healthy, strong man. Anyone who did succeed in leaving had to pay again to settle in a new place. A licence was needed before a man could sell one of his animals and the Lord of the Manor had first option over the sale; he was also able to pay less than the market rate for the beast, buying oxen at twopence and horses at fourpence less than the owner would have been able to obtain on the open market. A fee of sixpence had to be paid by a father to the Lord of the Manor when a daughter married. When one considers that a watchman would be paid one penny a day, ridding himself of a daughter could cost him a week's wages.

Farnham surnames of the same period often indicate the occupation of a person or sometimes the place where they lived: there are, for example, Henry le Butchyr, Peter le Carpenter and John Handybody, as well as Anastasia de Dupenhalle, John Wily, John de Hale and Terence de Compton.

Four

Pots, Wheat and Wool

W HEN THE MONKS from Waverley Abbey needed to visit their Bishop at Farnham Castle, they would walk into town via the present route of Old Compton Lane, Waverley Lane, Station Hill, Abbey Street, Longbridge, Downing Street and on up to the castle either via the main street or the back route through the present Argos store doorway and up Long Garden Walk. The townsfolk would see the monks in the white habits and wonder at what news they might be carrying to the Bishop, news which had been gleaned, perhaps, from pilgrims visiting the abbey. It is believed that the title of Sir Walter Scott's novel *Waverley* was inspired by this Cistercian monastery, which was the most important feature of Farnham for about four hundred years.

20 Abbey Street, Farnham, before Ashley Terrace, left, was demolished to make way for a wider Hickley's Corner junction, and the iron-monger's, from which the location derives its name, was also demolished. No speed restriction signs are really necessary, now: this thorough-fare has become a cul-de-sac. Persil, Skippers' sardines and Chiver's jellies are being advertised on the hoarding.

After the dissolution of the monasteries, much of the stone used in building Waverley Abbey was removed and used in Sir William More's house at Loseley. In 1536 the White family, who at that time were living in what is now Church Lane East, Aldershot, took over the 31 acres formerly farmed by the monks, on payment of 4s. 4d., an increase of just one penny in a period of over three hundred years.

Being on the route from Winchester to Canterbury, Farnham frequently saw pilgrims either going to pray at the tomb of St Swithun in Winchester or travelling in the opposite direction, to Kent, where they worshipped at the shrine of the murdered Archbishop Thomas à Becket (A.D. 1118–1170).

In his booklet *Farnham Castle*, published in 1947, Major A.G. Wade wrote that Farnham Castle stood on high ground

... immediately north of the crossroads—or rather the bottleneck of roads—where old (some say the oldest) roads in Britain meet ... Here the ancient trackways from Stonehenge, and the prehistoric metal mines of Cornwall, Wales and the Forest of Dean, join and pass through to the Channel ports of the Straits of Dover, to become the Roman way to Canterbury and to the Roman port of Richborough, and are met by the road from Winchester to London.

The area within the ancient Manor of Farnham is almost unique as regards the wide range of its archaeological material. Every period, from the lower Paleolithic to the present day, is represented within the bounds of the manor and all within a radius of some five miles from the castle.

In *The Old Road*, Hilaire Belloc writes: 'Farnham was always a place of capital importance. The fact that it was a meeting place of

21 This unusual view of Farnham Castle, taken more than a century ago, probably by John Henry Knight, is from an upper window of the former Working Men's or Castle Street Institute, now the Freemason's Hall, in Castle Street. It was administered by a charity from 1877 and in 1909 they offered it for sale as being suitable for a motor garage.

22 Charles Borelli (centre) featured in his own Christmas card in 1948. A belisha beacon once denoted a pedestrian crossing at the bottom of Castle Street, and both Spinning Wheel Antiques (formerly the second site of the *Goat's Head*) and Boots the Chemist are in the background. 'Miss Margaret' (Mrs. Wenham) can be seen peering into the shop doorway, right.

the roads that came from London and the Straits of Dover, necessarily made it a key to Southern England.'

Royal personages have always visited the town, both before and after Farnham Castle was built. The Saxon King Ceawlin (560-593) is the first monarch for whom there is plausible evidence of a visit. Elfrida Manning, one of Farnham's leading authorities on the Saxon period, stated that during Ceawlin's 'long and comparatively peaceful reign there is archaeological evidence that there was further penetration by the Saxons into the remoter parts of Surrey. In Farnham a group of weaving huts of approximately this date was discovered

near the river crossing at Longbridge, so that we can probably date the first Saxon settlement of Farnham to Ceawlin's reign.'

There is positive evidence of Caedwalla, King of Wessex A.D. 685-688, visiting, and it was he who gave the land at Farnham to the Church. It is believed that in 1066 William of Normandy came through Farnham, and that he received the submission of the ancient Saxon capital of Winchester.

King John, who reigned from 1199-1216, is recorded as having visited Farnham 18 times. He is known to have loved hunting and it was presumably for this reason that he came here so frequently. Quoting from *Medieval Farnham*, by Father E. Robo, published in 1935, Leni Grosset, in a Farnham and District Museum Newsletter writes:

> Hunting was the great pastime of King John. When he was in Farnham in 1208-9, some of his horses were kept at the castle from November 1st to January 14th and this cost the bishop the sum of 13s. 10d. while a soldier who came for the gerfalcons of the lord king received 6d. In 1210-11 the king's horse was stabled at the castle for seven weeks at a cost of 2s. a week ... Expenses of two men looking after the king's horses during 18 days: 4s. 8d. ... Shoeing the horses: 7d.

Miss Grosset continues:

> Though there are no records of the number of deer he brought down, it must have been considerable judging by the large quantities of salt (for preserving the venison) bought on the occasion of King John's visit in 1210. In medieval times it was customary for the king and his retinue to journey the rounds of his castles and manors—not necessarily from choice but because it was easier to go where the food was produced than to transport the food itself.

Henry III was a guest at Farnham Castle at least 14 times, but the occasion which he probably remembered best was his visit in March 1217 when he was about nine years of age. This was the time when William Marshall, the Earl of Pembroke, recaptured the castle from the small contingent of the French army belonging to Louis, Dauphin of France, who had occupied it for nine months.

Edward I is recorded as having been a visitor to the castle at least nine times; Edward III made several visits and on one occasion he brought his wife with him; Richard III stayed at Farnham Castle for two days in 1483.

Henry VII's son and heir, Prince Arthur, was born in September 1486 and the baby was baptised by Bishop Courtenay, Bishop of Winchester, in 1487. Although it is not recorded in public documents, it is almost certain that King Henry VII and his Queen,

Elizabeth of York, visited the baby when he was being nursed at the castle for much of the first year of his life. Arthur's brother, the future King Henry VIII, was born four years later and probably spent some time during his boyhood at the castle, because his godfather was Bishop Fox, Bishop of Winchester from 1500-28.

We know Henry VIII was at Farnham Castle when he was 16 years old because Father Robo records that Henry wrote a letter to Thomas Wolsey, dated 'Farnham Castle at 11 o'clock of the night', which concerned a request made by ambassadors for further aid to the Emperor Maximilian I.

In towns and villages throughout this country, a market place is frequently found at the place where roads cross. Around this meeting and crossing spot towns grew up and thus it has been in Farnham, despite the fact that today the market consists of little more than a greengrocery stall, a florist's van and a second-hand furniture dealer's tarpaulin. The old Harrow Way became the pilgrims' way, and Mrs. Newnam, in *The Story of Farnham*, cites as evidence that at least one pilgrim came through the town centre, a medieval pilgrim's green pottery bottle found buried near Lion and Lamb Yard.

Farnham received a new Charter in 1566, in which the people were given responsibility for their own trade and behaviour. Two bailiffs, John Clark, a builder, and Robert Quynby (who was buried four years later in the chancel of St Andrew's Church), were appointed by the Bishop, along with 12 burgesses, who held courts every three weeks in the Market House. They dealt with misdemeanours such as trespass, assault and debt. Examples of fines they exacted include that of 3s. 4d. for any inhabitant who did not clean his sinks and gutters, and 4d. for using dishonest and unfitting words to a constable.

Maps of Surrey were being made from proper measurements, and on them landmarks such as the castle, park, river and the bridge across it can be seen. Houses in West Street, East Street, Downing Street and Abbey Street (there were five here in 1516) can be recognised and some buildings, such as that which now houses Guitar Village, in West Street, and others in Castle Street can still be seen today.

In 1566 a market house was built at the bottom of Castle Street and a model of it can be seen in the Museum of Farnham. It was demolished 300 years later but the timber was not wasted. Much of it was used in the construction of a pair of houses in East Street built with a roundel representing the place where the clock had been, and with bargeboards under the eaves giving an appearance similar to the front of the market house from which the timbers had been obtained. The town was beginning to grow quite rapidly now, and the occupations of its citizens becoming more diverse. Clay from Farnham Park and other areas, including Wrecclesham and Elstead, was being dug for pots and some of Farnham's famous greenware was ordered for the Temple in London.

Farnham was well known in the capital, not only because of the monastery at Waverley and the castle, home of the Bishop of Winchester, but also because the beamed roof of Westminster Hall had been constructed here in 1395. It is believed that the work involved in this feat of medieval craftsmanship was carried out in what is now known as Timber Close, off West Street, and for over 500 years it was the largest, unsupported roof structure in Europe. It is still a familiar sight to members of parliament today.

During the 17th century the sound of Farnham's church bells was heard frequently— outside the regular calls to worship. Mrs. Newnam records that they were rung when Queen Elizabeth I passed through *en route* from London to Winchester; 'when the rebels were beaten; when my Lord Bishop came out of the West; when the King was proclaimed; for ringing the Bishop home; for joy the siege was beat off at Londonderry, and in 1716 when

23 The house in East Street which once housed the offices of Phillimore and Co. Ltd., the publisher of this volume. All its archive material was stored in an outhouse to the rear of the building and the offices were in the house which, a century earlier, had the *Eagle*, one of Farnham's many hostelries, as its neighbour.

the King came from Hanover'. The most unusual of the events to be commemorated by bell-ringing in Farnham must surely be the 'beating off of a siege' in Londonderry!

Farnham became a very popular wheat market at about this time. Wheat grown in Hampshire and Sussex, and intended for the London market, was sent by road through Farnham. It was a good halfway point, and London traders would travel here to make arrangements about its final destination. Great wagons, each pulled by six horses, arrived from places such as Alresford, Alton, Petersfield and Chichester. Wagons were kept safe overnight in the many yards of the town, which are still

24 Alice Holt Forest, where the Romans had pottery kilns and from which much of the wood for the roof of Westminster Hall came, was a popular place of work in the Victorian era. These men, and boys, from Frensham were photographed by J.H. Dodman, a photographer in the village, who also published and sold this postcard.

25 Queen Elizabeth I and the Duke of Norfolk both visited Farnham Castle and were characters in the *Farnham Pageant*, written by Farnham's rector, Rev. Neville Lovett. It was first performed in 1910. In the second production, in 1930, Miss J. Nicholson and Colonel Coxon played the Queen and Duke, as photographed left at the dress rehearsal. The pageant was performed again in 1950 and 1987.

in existence and which are considered in more detail in a later chapter.

Some of the corn was ground into flour before it went on to London. This work, combined with the provision of lodging places for the waggoners, bread to feed them and ale to slake their thirst, meant that there were several lucrative means of making a livelihood here at that time.

A few of the people who made money in the town returned some of it by helping the poor, and in 1619 several almshouses were built by Andrew Windsor, in Castle Street, for the habitation of eight poor, honest, old, impotent persons. These remained as homes for eight people until the 1980s, when they were gutted inside and turned into four dwellings. At about the same time another group of almshouses

was built in the gardens behind the original units.

Farnham was also known for its cloth. Until the dissolution of Waverley Abbey, the monks were recognised for the cloth they made using the wool sheared from their vast flocks. Although there is not a great deal of information about this industry for historians today, evidence of clothmaking and clothiers is continuous for at least 200 years, from 1500 to 1711. There were 15 clothiers in Farnham in 1574, for example, and 797 pieces of cloth in the market. Five years earlier, in 1569, some Farnham men had been fined for stretching kersey (the name given to the woollen cloth made here) from 18 to 20 yards. In 1711 John Luffe is recorded as having paid 30 shillings for a licence to dig Fullers Earth at

26 Early 17th-century cottages in Castle Street, built in 1619 as a home for eight poor, honest, old, impotent persons, by benefactor Andrew Windsor. In 1989 they were converted into four dwellings. The plane trees were planted in 1897, to commemorate Queen Victoria's Diamond Jubilee.

27 Unlike today, this Tudor building, for many years the second site of the *Goat's Head*, had, at one time, two-way traffic past its frontage, as the motor cycle shows. Presumably the bike's owner had popped inside the Spinning Wheel antiques shop to find a bygone piece. Today, regrettably, the vases on display outside would be vandalised or stolen.

Wishanger, Churt. This was used at the fulling mill to soak the woollen material in until it was thick enough to be windproof before it was worked. Nigel Temple, in *Farnham Buildings and People*, believes there is some evidence that 40 The Borough, today Bally Shoes and formerly the *Goat's Head* public house, was once the home of a cloth merchant. However, by the end of the 17th century John Aubrey could not find a single clothier in Farnham. Wheat marketing continued and until the last quarter of the 18th century it was the principal way in which the town's inhabitants made their money.

The group of bailiffs and burgesses, first appointed in 1566 and drawn from the leading merchants, had become so powerful they were able to afford to pay to have lectures, by Puritans, given at the weekly market. These lectures were supposed to make up for the lack of preaching from the Anglican vicar in the town who, from 1623, was a man named Paul Clapham. Mr. Clapham was a former chaplain to the Bishop of Winchester; he received £12 a year for market tolls from the people of Farnham and he also held the rectory at Martyr Worthy, near Winchester. Later the people at Martyr Worthy, and in Farnham, cited him for scandalous behaviour. From 1639-48 the Puritan lecturer, Mr. H. Duncomb, was allowed to move in to the vacant vicarage near the parish church.

Five

Queen Elizabeth Slept Here

WHEN HENRY VIII was in residence at the castle it is certain that he took advantage of the surrounding park, teeming with red and fallow deer, to go hunting, and it is possible that on one of these sporting rides he lost a gold and sapphire pin from his hat. Pins similar to one which was found by Ian Fletcher, and valued at up to £30,000, can be seen in a portrait of the King painted by Holbein. Mr. Fletcher was a visitor to the town who, in all innocence, used his metal detector in the upper part of the park near the present Folly Hill in 1992, against Waverley Borough Council's bye-laws. Despite his following all the correct procedures and originally being awarded possession of the pin in the High Court, Waverley Borough Council appealed against the High Court ruling and judgement was given against the finder. He also had to pay the court costs and the case was high-lighted in a Channel Four television documentary programme, *Joe Public*, screened in November 1998.

The pin was on display in the Museum of Farnham in a reinforced glass showcase for only a few months before a burglary, in the early hours of 27 January 1999, resulted in the theft of the delicate piece of jewellery, which measured just over one inch in diameter.

In 1531 Farnham Castle was without a clerical occupant for a year because Henry VIII held the post of Bishop of Winchester vacant for his own ends on the death of Cardinal Wolsey in November 1530. King Henry was at the castle on 31 July and 3 August 1531 and from 13-17 September 1535.

In an article for the Farnham and District Museum Society Newsletter in 1977, Freda Midgley records that Mary Tudor spent time at Farnham Castle in 1554, on her progress to Winchester Cathedral for her marriage to Philip of Spain. She reached Farnham on 22 June and probably spent the following three weeks there, hunting, which was fashionable for women as well as men in those days, playing her lute or doing her embroidery (she was a skilled needlewoman), before leaving for Winchester on 11 July. She married Philip of Spain, in Winchester Cathedral, on the evening of 23 July.

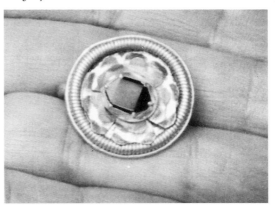

28 This Tudor gold and sapphire pin was found in Farnham Park in 1992, by Ian Fletcher, a visitor to the town. It has been linked to Henry VIII (he is wearing similar pins in his hat in a Holbein painting). The subject of a lengthy legal battle, the pin, worth £30,000, eventually became the property of Waverley Borough Council but was stolen in 1999.

29 Although the Rev. Neville Lovett admits that the tableau, dated A.D. 1530, in his *Farnham Pageant*, 'is founded rather on possibility than on ascertained fact', Cardinal Wolsey was Bishop of Winchester from 1528–30. In the 1930 production, Cardinal Wolsey (H.C. Patrick, the town's principal undertaker) is guarded by F.W. Gohery, H.R. James, S.H. Budd and E.W. Larmer.

30 This postcard, printed in Saxony in the early 20th century, shows part of the Great Hall, Farnham Castle. The fireplace, with the legend *A Dieu foy. Aux amis foyer* (To God my faith, to my friends my hearth) incised beneath the mantelpiece, still remains to welcome those who partake of the Venison Dinner, held annually in November in this room.

Queen Elizabeth I made at least six visits to Farnham Castle, and on one of these, which took place in August 1569, when Robert Horne was nine years into his 20-year period as Bishop of Winchester, she is reputed to have warned the Duke of Norfolk, while conferring with him about the marriage of Mary Queen of Scots, that he should 'be very careful on what pillow he laid his head'. Queen Elizabeth spent the summer of 1583 at the castle, when John Watson, a doctor of medicine, was Bishop. She honoured Bishop Thomas Cooper with her presence there in August 1591, and she was the esteemed guest of Bishop Thomas Bilson in 1601.

King James leased the hunting rights at Farnham 'for the lifetime' of Bishop Bilson, which cost him £106 6s. 10d. a year. During the period of lease there was a fire in the stables at the castle, in 1609, the cause of which is believed to have been a fallen candle. A number of horses were burned to death and some which were with foal miscarried; harness and saddles were lost. Despite what must have been a serious incident a letter written by the Earl of Worcester to the Earl of Salisbury at that time records that 'neither King, Queen or Prince slept the worse or ever waked until the morning in due time'.

James I visited Farnham frequently, possibly because he was treated so well at the castle, particularly in 1620 when it is said he was entertained, at great expense, by Bishop Andrewes, who apparently gave 'as beautiful and great an entertainment as ever a King received from a subject'.

Charles I's visit to the town was in less auspicious circumstances. A rebellion in Ireland in 1641 finally sparked off a war between King Charles and his Parliament. The Catholic population in Ireland rose against the English—who had crossed the Irish Sea to settle in their country—and their government. Hundreds of Protestants who had settled there were killed, but Parliament refused to allow an army to go to Ireland unless it was under the command of

people they chose rather than under the jurisdiction of the King. The issue turned into a power struggle. The House of Commons produced a document which the King would not sign. Then the King tried to arrest five of the ringleaders in the House of Commons and one in the House of Lords, but they claimed sanctuary in the City of London and its gates were shut against the King.

In the summer of 1642 King Charles I went to York to raise support against Parliament and when the Royal Standard was raised at Nottingham on 22 August 1642, this ancient and symbolic gesture of a call to arms was the start of a period of civil war.

The effect the English Civil War had on Farnham is well recorded and documented in *Farnham During the Civil Wars and Interregnum 1642-1660*, by D.E. Hall and F. Gretton. The Parliamentarians, led by Colonel Sir William Waller, captured Farnham Castle in 1642 from Royalist hands. In July 1643 a regiment of foot soldiers, under Colonel Samuel Jones, was ordered into Surrey and their headquarters was to be in Farnham. The Farnham Regiment of Foot was known as the 'Greencoats' from the colour of their uniform jackets. Their company ensigns were white. All the details of this group have been recorded in *The Farnham Greencoats* by Lawrence Spring and Derek Hall, and for students of this period the two booklets mentioned above are to be recommended.

A green-glazed plaque on the wall of Vernon House, West Street, now part of Farnham Library, states that 'Charles I stayed here on the night of 20 December 1648.' The King, now captive, was on his way from the Isle of Wight to London and to his eventual beheading a month later, on 29 January 1649. In an article written for the Farnham and District Museum Newsletter in June 1990, Leni Grosset highlights an interesting aspect of the execution. According to Thomas Herbert, who was an eye-witness to the beheading, the event took place on 29 January

31 Vernon House, West Street, where King Charles I stayed for one night in 1648. An earlier name was Culver Hall and part of it was built in the first quarter of the 17th century. The street façade is probably from 1721—the date on the rainwater heads. It is likely that the adjoining house, No.29, with its smoke hole, is the old Timber Hall.

32 Little could Charles I have imagined, when this medal was struck for his coronation in 1626, that 23 years later, in January 1649, he would lose his head.

1648, a year earlier than the plaque suggests. In his memoirs, Thomas Herbert (later Sir) also includes the following details: 'The girdle or circumscription of Capitall Letters in Lead putt about the Coffin had only these words— KING CHARLES 1648.' Miss Grosset concludes that the King was apparently sentenced and executed a year before he stayed in Farnham. The plaque, however, is not incorrect. Miss Grosset goes on to explain how,

before the calendar reform in 1752, the years were counted from Lady Day, which fell on 25 March, making all of January, February and up to 24 March fall in the year previous to the one we would consider them to fall in today. This change in the calendar thus clears up the mystery.

The above illustration is only one example of the difficulty historians have with dating before the statute reforming the calendar which

33 Castle Street about a century ago, with what appears to be a three-wheeled goat cart and a window cleaner's two-wheeled mode of transport. No other vehicle is in sight. Farnham Steam Bakery is on the right, chimneys can be seen on Fox's Tower, and two lamp standards appear to be almost in the middle of the road.

is often known as the Chesterfield Act. The most relevant portion read:

> Pursuant to Statute 24 George II c.23, 1751 it was enacted that throughout all His Majesty's Dominions in Europe, Asia, Africa and America, the supputation according to the year of our Lord began on 25 March shall not be used again after the last day of December 1751, and the first day of January next following shall be reckoned and numbered in the same order; and the feast of Easter and other moveable feasts thereon depending shall be ascertained according to the same method as they are now, until the 2 September 1752 (Wednesday). That the natural day immediately following 2 September 1752 shall be called and reckoned the 14th day of September (Thursday), omitting the eleven mediate nominal days of the common calendar.

This apparent loss of 11 days caused great anger and many problems, particularly where monthly wages and rents were concerned, and mobs rioting in the streets shouted 'Give us back our eleven days'. The *Gentlemen's Magazine* carried a letter signed 'Your most perplexed and confused humble servant, R.R.' in its issue dated 15 September 1752.

> ... How is all this? I desire to know plainly and truly! I went to bed last night, it was Wednesday Sept.2, and the first thing I call my eye upon this morning at the top of your paper was Thursday, Sept. 14. I did not go to bed till between one and two. Have I slept away 11 days in 7 hours, or how is it? For my part I don't find I'm any more refresh'd than after a common night's sleep.

Local people reading the works of Derek Hall concerning the Civil Wars in Farnham, should note that Mr. Hall uses the pre-1752 dates for the day of the month but the year as in the post-1752 calendar.

The foregoing all adds up to the fact that Charles I did enjoy Farnham hospitality in 1648, and was beheaded a month later, in 1649, ironically having been tried in Westminster Hall, the roof of which was made in Farnham about 250 years earlier. As a prisoner, he had no money with which to repay his Farnham host, Sir Henry Vernon, so he gave the blind man his morning cap. This is made from blue silk covered with gold and silver embroidery and can be seen in the Museum of Farnham. Beneath the case in which it is displayed is part of a Vernon family will in which the cap is mentioned. It would seem that the writer of the will did not hold the cap in very high esteem, suggesting that after all his family had done in the Royalist cause, all they received for their pains was an old hat!

Charles II was a frequent visitor, both when Bishop Duppa, who had been his tutor, held the bishopric from 1660-2, and when Bishop Morley held the See. Charles II was so frequent a visitor to Bishop Morley that he allegedly earned this rebuke from the cleric: 'The king and his brother abused my hospitality at Farnham ... and used the Castle as an Inn.'

Farnham historian Gwen Ware states that there is no record of James II visiting the town when he was King, although she says that there is an unhappy link between the House of Stuart and Farnham Castle. In the castle dungeons, scratched on a wall in an educated hand, is the name JAMYS. Gwen Ware conjectures that the writing could possibly be that of James, Duke of Monmouth, Charles II's illegitimate son, who was brought through Farnham after his defeat at the Battle of Sedgemoor in 1685, on his way to execution.

The townsfolk of Farnham must have been very surprised one Monday morning in 1778, when at around 11 o'clock, unheralded by the ringing of church bells since it was not a state occasion, they saw King George III driving Queen Charlotte in a light phaeton up Castle Street. Following the royal couple came four horse-drawn coaches and a retinue of servants. The visit was an informal one: at the suggestion of one of the Bishop's staff, a Mr. Buller, the King, Queen and their 12 children were calling to wish Bishop Thomas greetings on his 81st birthday.

At the time of this visit, Hester Chapone, a niece of the Bishop and a writer on moral subjects, was staying at the castle. Her *Letters on the Improvement of the Mind, Religion, Geography and Domestic Economy* was, apparently, greatly admired, and George III's eldest daughter, the Princess Royal, had read it. Mrs. Chapone was flattered when Queen Charlotte said to her, regarding the Princess Royal: 'This is a young lady who I hope has profited much by your instructions. She has read them once and will read them oftener.' Mrs. Chapone considered that the Princess 'had a very modest air … a sweet countenance and simple, unaffected manners.' She also wrote of the future King William IV,

> I was pleased with all the princes but particularly with Prince William, who is little of his age but so sensible and engaging that he won the Bishop's heart; to whom he particularly attached himself, and would stay with him while all the rest ran about the house. His conversation was surprisingly manly and clever of his age.

The information about the birthday visit to Bishop Thomas was compiled by Freda Midgley from information in a book by John Cole published in 1839. Unfortunately, the extracts from Mrs. Chapone's letters break off before the visit ends, and we can only guess how the townspeople viewed the procession of King, Queen, children, babies, nursemaids, governesses and all the other members of the party making their way down Castle Street again for their return journey to Windsor Castle.

Queen Victoria also paid a surprise visit to Farnham Castle, in May 1860. Accompanied by Prince Albert, the Queen, then aged 41, arrived on horseback at the Hoghatch entrance to Farnham Park, having ridden over from Aldershot where she had been inspecting the troops. Princess Alice and her attendants, who travelled in carriages, entered the park through the London Gate and then travelled along The Avenue until they met the Queen's party at the garden gate of the castle, where they were all welcomed by Bishop Sumner. He showed them over parts of the castle, and they spent some time in the Norman Chapel before returning to Aldershot via East Street. Two narrow roads in

34 An Edwardian view looking east along East Street, with Farnham Motor Works on the left and in the far distance the Farnham Motor Company Garage. The white sign, centre left, is for the *Green Man*. This faces the *Marlborough Head*, rebuilt in the 1920s, and in the right foreground Mr. Kimbell displays his name outside the *Royal Deer*.

35   A fifth form class at Farnham Grammar School in 1965. The boys are in a temporary hut, situated near the playground, and include Bob Simpson, John Hughes, Peter 'Pilgrim' Miller and 'Rusty' Moorcroft. The blazer badge, familiar to every ex-pupil this century, can clearly be seen on the blazer pocket of the boy sharing a desk at the front.

Hale, along which the Queen had ridden on her outward journey, were named Queen's Lane and Queen's Road. For some while consideration was given to renaming East Street as Queen Street, in honour of the monarch's passage through it, and a hostelry on the corner of East Street and Bear Lane became known as *Queen Street Tavern*. However, both town names were short-lived, and the street remained what it had been for centuries, East Street, until part of it was renamed The Woolmead following demolition in the 1960s of a row of buildings on the street's north side.

William 'Billy' Stroud, for many years a master at Farnham Grammar School, recorded an amusing incident which took place as the royal party came down Castle Street on their return to Aldershot. He wrote,

Now there was a menagerie in the street at the time just opposite Tily's [now Caffe Uno]. The crowd outside the show recognized the Royal party and broke into loud cheers. Someone in the menagerie shouted 'A lion has got loose.' Mothers caught their children up and made for the exit, only to find out, when they got outside, the cause of the shouting. When the Queen had passed these frightened people wanted to go back but were told by the door-keeper that they must pay again.

The 20th century is notable for its lack of royal visitors to Farnham, although Princess Anne had lunch at Farnham Castle in July 1982, when she was at a function there with ex-Farnham Girls' Grammar School pupil, Liza Goddard, and her husband, Alvin Stardust, to raise money for the Save the Children Fund.

36 Mary Joynes, right, started a choir for children in 1948. This is one of their first photographs, taken in the Congregational Church Hall at a time when most girls wore hair ribbons and small boys wore ties. The choir, under different names and age groups, ran for 39 years until 1987, when Mary retired.

37 Twenty-five years ago the 1st Farnham Girl Guides picked blackberries to make jam to be sold for charity. Bryan Sell, back left, accepted money for Bell's Piece Cheshire Home and Michael Nightingale for *Talking Newspaper*. Amongst the Guides are Joanna Kelsey, now a silversmith, and Teresa Forward, who is married to Alan, a member of the Thorpe family of cricketers.

38   A somewhat damaged photograph taken about thirty years ago of Brownies in Farnham saying goodbye to Brown Owl, Mrs. Philipson-Stow, centre, on her last night in office. Mrs. Philipson-Stow lived in a house in St Andrew's Churchyard. Only the sixer badges remain as similar parts of the uniform today.

She also took part in the Frensham Horse Trials, in 1981. Princess Margaret visited the former Redgrave Theatre on two occasions, in June 1974, and again in 1984. Queen Elizabeth II went down Upper Weybourne Lane in the 1960s, and Brownies stood on the forecourt of the *Royal Arms* public house to wave to her. Prince Andrew attended the wedding, at Frensham, of a Gordonstoun school friend, Nicholas Oliver, who married Sara Jane McCann in June 1981. All such visits were brief, though, and although costly in terms of policing and security did not represent a personal loss to any individual so did not warrant rebukes such as that given by Bishop Morley to Charles II.

Six

Kings, Queens and Bishops

ALTHOUGH FARNHAM DEVELOPED because of its location at a crossroads, it is unlikely that it would have been such an important place had it not been for the fact that both the castle, home of the Bishops of Winchester for 803 years, and Waverley Abbey, the first Cistercian monastery in this country, were built here, within two miles of each other.

Bishop of Winchester Henry de Blois (1129-71) was the original builder of Farnham Castle, during the reign of King Henry I (1100-35). He was a grandson of William the Conqueror and a younger brother of King Stephen (1135-54), which meant that when Stephen ruled the land his brother had control of one of the most important clerical positions in the country. In all, Henry de Blois built six castles and he also founded the Hospital of St Cross, in Winchester, in 1136. A street in Farnham has been named St Cross Road, to record this refuge.

Thoroughfares in the town named after Bishops of Winchester include Thorold Road, Morley Road, Wykeham Road, Beaufort Road, Ryle Road, Talbot Road, Courtenay Road and Sumner Road.

Bishop Henry de Blois laboured tirelessly for the good of his diocese during his time at the castle, which was under three reigns, Henry II coming to the throne in 1154.

Richard Toclive (1174-88) was elected by monks after the See of Winchester had been vacant for three years following Henry's death. Like his predecessor, Richard also founded a hospital at Winchester, dedicated to St Mary Magdalene, but it was pulled down in 1788. His period of office ended a year before Richard I ascended the throne.

39 Representing Bishop and Mrs. Sumner in the 1930 *Farnham Pageant* are the Rev. C. Sumner Stooks and Mrs. A. Ball. Bishop Sumner came to Farnham in 1828 and died here in 1874. He is known as the 'last of the Prince Bishops' because, on his death, the extensive properties belonging to the See were transferred to the ecclesiastical commissioners for administration.

From 1188 to 1204, Godfrey de Lucy was Bishop of Winchester. This man was an architect of repute and had the retro-choir in Winchester Cathedral built during his term of office. He also saw the crowning of King John (1199-1216).

Peter de la Roche (or de Rupibus) held the See from 1205-38 and was consecrated Bishop of Winchester in Rome. Much against the wishes of English nobles, Peter became the Grand Justiciary of England and was guardian of King Henry III, who was only nine years old when he ascended the throne. Peter de la Roche fought in the Holy Land in 1226; he also built a monastery at Selborne which was described by the naturalist and author, Gilbert White. In June 1238, the Bishop died at Farnham Castle, a place he had called home for 33 years.

The other Bishops of Winchester during the reign of Henry III were William de Raleigh (1244-49), Ethelmar (or Aylmer) de Valence (1250-61), John of Exeter, otherwise known as John Gervase (1262-68), and Nicholas of Ely (1268-80). Ethelmar de Valence was half-brother to King Henry III and he freed the Farnham bondmen in 1256. John of Exeter, who assisted Simon de Montfort in the Civil War, died in Rome, whilst Nicholas of Ely, who was both Lord Chancellor and Lord High Treasurer, was buried much closer to home, at Waverley Abbey, in Moor Park. Nicholas of Ely's bishopric extended into the reign of King Edward I (1272-1307). He was succeeded by John de Pontissara (1282-1304) who built a college at Winchester, St Elizabeth of Hungary, and who was also Chancellor of Oxford University and Professor of Civil Law at Modena.

Two years before the end of Edward's reign, Henry Woodlock (1305-16) became Bishop of Winchester. He was a former Prior of St Swithun's Monastery and it was he who crowned the next monarch, Edward II, in 1307. During Edward's reign (1307-27), three other people also took responsibility for the See of

Winchester, namely John Sandale (1316-19), Reginald Asser (1320-23) and John Stratford (1323-33). Adam Orleton (1333-45) was Bishop of Winchester when Edward III (1327-77) ascended the throne. He was succeeded by William Edington (1346-66), a man who did much to re-model the nave of Winchester Cathedral at the same time as being Chancellor of England.

Then came William of Wykeham (1367-1404), whose term of office took place under two more sovereigns, Richard II (1377-99) and Henry IV (1399-1413).William was educated at Winchester and Oxford and was presented to King Edward III when he was 23 years old, having no advantages other than great architectural skills. During the following years he rose rapidly through a variety of important positions, until he became Bishop of Winchester and Lord High Chancellor of England in 1367.

He was responsible for the construction of the Round Tower at Windsor Castle as well as the Eastern Ward, plus a college for the Order of the Garter (situated close to St George's Chapel). One of the towers still bears the inscription: 'This made Wykeham'. In 1361 he commenced the building of Queensborough Castle, although it was demolished in 1650. He is also said to have been responsible for rebuilding five other castles and undertook the building of New College, Oxford, which he opened in April 1386. He built Winchester College in 1382 and in 1394 took upon himself the massive task of the reformation of Winchester Cathedral. Bishop Wykeham was responsible for the image of the British public school, still prevalent in Britain today, by his building of Winchester College. He became a very rich man but spent much of his money on the promotion of learning. Unusually for his time, he lived to the ripe old age of 80 years.

Henry of Beaufort (Bishop of Winchester 1405-47) was extremely rich, as well as being the uncle of King Henry V (to whom he lent

£20,000); he rebuilt the Hospital of St Cross and spent vast sums on debtors' prisons in London. He was Bishop of Winchester for a further 14 years under Henry VI, before he was succeeded by William of Waynflete (1447-86), the man responsible for building the brick tower of Farnham Castle, now known as Fox's Tower. A very well-educated man, he also founded Magdalen College, Oxford.

William Waynflete's period as bishop also covered the reigns of King Edward IV (1461-83), Edward V (1483) (the 'boy king' who was never crowned in Westminster Abbey, as his ancestors had been, but was murdered with his brother Richard), Richard III (1483-85), and extended one year into the reign of King Henry VII (1485-1509). He was succeeded by Peter Courtenay (1486-92), who was followed by Thomas Langton (1493-1500), a bishop who died from the plague.

After the death of Thomas Langton, Richard Fox (1500-28) became Bishop, and although he spent the first nine years under Henry VII, he also served under King Henry VIII (1509-47), to whom he was godfather. In later life Bishop Fox was blind, but this did not stop him carrying out many works of restoration, including the tower built by William of Waynflete. Much of the work in the Lady Chapel at Winchester was due to Bishop Fox, and he was also the joint founder of Corpus Christi College in Oxford. The steps leading to the fortress on the hill were designed so that a blind man could walk to and from the town unaided: there are sets of seven steps with seven paces in between each set. Even today, on leaving the castle in the dark, if the street light is not functioning, sighted as well as blind people find it comforting to know that they can reach street level in safety as long as they are able to count to seven.

Thomas Wolsey (1528-30), cardinal and chancellor, was responsible for the See of Winchester after Richard Fox and he, in turn, was succeeded by Stephen Gardiner (who held the office on two occasions, 1531-51 and

40 A cleric, Canon Girling, played the part of Bishop Fox, right, and R.B. Varey took the role of his chaplain, in the *Farnham Pageant* of 1930. Fox, Bishop of Winchester from 1501-28, was blind in his declining years. Towards the end of his life clouds were gathering over the Church and they burst in the storm of the Reformation.

1553-5). Stephen Gardiner had considerable personal contact with the royal family, and he not only advised King Henry VIII in his divorce proceedings against Katherine of Aragon but he also crowned Mary I, in 1553, and performed the marriage ceremony between Mary and Philip of Spain.

Stephen Gardiner was still Bishop of Winchester when King Edward VI (1547-53) ascended the throne, but he was deprived of this position by that monarch in 1551, and John Ponet (or Poynet) (1551-53) was appointed Bishop in Stephen's stead. However, once she became Queen, Mary re-instated Stephen Gardiner. John Ponet died in Strasbourg in 1556.

From 1556-9, John White, who had been born in Farnham, was Bishop under Mary, but he was deposed by Queen Elizabeth I (1558-1603) in 1559, and was succeeded by Robert Horne (1560-80), Doctor of Medicine John Watson (1580-3), Thomas Cooper (1583-94), William Wickham (1595), William Day (1596) and Thomas Bilson (1596-1616).

William Wickham claimed descent from William of Wykeham, although he was actually a member of a different family, and he died in Southwark before he ever moved to Winchester, so it is possible that he never set foot inside Farnham Castle. He pronounced the oration for Mary Queen of Scots at her funeral. William Day, brother-in-law of William Wickham, was another of the short-lived holders of the See, being in office for just one year. Thomas Bilson was the author of many books, perhaps the first of the 'Farnham authors', the prolific group of writers who have found inspiration in this town.

He was still Bishop of Winchester when King James I (1603-25) ascended the throne. James Montague (1616-18) succeeded Thomas and was followed by Lancelot Andrewes (1619-26). Lancelot was known as the 'Saintly Bishop' and was often called 'an angel in the pulpit'. It is said that he held great influence over King James and was also a powerful preacher.

Lancelot's successor was Richard Neile (1627-31), the son of a tallow chandler. It is interesting to note that not all Bishops of Winchester were from wealthy and impressive backgrounds. To be the son of a man who melted down the fat from sheep and oxen to make candles, can hardly be said to be of a family of high standing. Walter Curle (1632-47) was Richard Neile's successor.

Charles II, having been crowned in Scotland in 1651, was crowned again at Westminster on 13 April 1661, and in the same year Brian Duppa (1660-2) became Bishop of Winchester. He had been tutor to both the King and his brother. Bishop Duppa had earlier been chaplain to King Charles I and had given

him much comfort when the King was in prison. Brian Duppa is also mentioned in the diaries of Samuel Pepys in entries for 29 July and 4 October 1660.

The next Bishop of Winchester, George Morley (1662-84), had also been a supporter of King Charles I. Farnham Grammar School, which had been founded in 1351, received several benefices from Bishop Morley, and when a custom-built school was constructed, in 1904, for the grammar school boys of Farnham, the road in which it was built was later named after this benefactor. Following the ravages which had taken place on Farnham Castle during the Civil War, it was in dire need of repair, and Bishop Morley spent £30,000 on this work. He also founded the College for Widows of the Clergy, near Winchester Cathedral. He was an octogenarian when he passed away and, like Peter de la Roche, 450 years earlier, he died at Farnham Castle.

Peter Mews, who held the See of Winchester from 1684-1706, knew King Charles II well and had followed him to Flanders when the latter fled from London in 1648. After he became Bishop of Winchester, Peter Mews took part in the Battle of Sedgemoor and was wounded. Mews was Lord of the Manor in Farnham during the last year of the reign of King Charles II, throughout the reign of King James II (1685-8), during that of William and Mary (1688-1702) and for four years while Queen Anne (1702-14) was on the throne. Jonathan Trelawny, baronet (1707-1721) succeeded him at Winchester, although as Bishop of Bristol, in 1688, he was one of seven bishops who had been tried in the reign of King James II.

Jonathan Trelawny continued into the reign of King George I (1714-27). From 1721-3, Charles Trimnell held the See, and he also died at Farnham Castle. During the reigns of King George II (1727-60) and George III (1760-1820), four bishops held the See of Winchester: Richard Willis (1723-34),

41 A line-up of Old Boys from the town's oldest educational establishment, Farnham Grammar School (in existence from at least the 17th century), at an Old Farnhamians' Dinner. They include John Crotty, left, Eddie Glynn, centre, John Aylwin to his left, Bill Bodkin, and the school's second-to-last headmaster, George Baxter, right. It became Farnham Sixth Form College in 1974.

42 Two of the magnificent cedars at Farnham Castle which, as seeds, were brought back from the Lebanon and planted by Mrs. Brownlow North, wife of the Bishop of Winchester who held the See from 1781–1820. Only one now remains; its partner came down in gales in the early 1990s.

Benjamin Hoadley (1734-61), John Thomas (1761-81) and Hon. Brownlow North (1781-1820). Bishop Hoadley had been chaplain to King George I and Bishop Thomas had tutored George III. Bishop North spent £6,000 on Farnham Castle and his wife brought seeds from cedar trees back to Farnham from the Lebanon. Despite the exposed location, several trees grew and one can still be seen today.

George Pretyman Tomline became Bishop of Winchester in 1820, the year George IV (1820-30) ascended the throne. Bishop Tomline was the author of several theological works. Three years before William IV became king (1830-37), Charles Sumner, probably the best-loved of all the bishops of Winchester, moved into Farnham Castle. From 1827-69, Bishop Sumner did much to help the working man and woman in the town and paid to have a school built at Upper Hale as well as a church at Lower Hale, for the benefit of the mainly poor population in that

area. These people were trying to eke out a meagre existence on the common land and carrying out tasks such as washing for the military personnel at Aldershot. Bishop Sumner is buried in the churchyard at St John's, Hale, having chosen this as his final resting place rather than Winchester which was his right as a Bishop of that See. In 1821 Bishop Sumner had been private chaplain to King George IV, at Windsor.

In 1837, the young Princess Victoria took up the reins of Queen, and Samuel Wilberforce, son of William Wilberforce, the emancipator and first cousin to Charles Sumner, became Bishop of Winchester for just four years, from 1869-73. However, Wilberforce never lived at Farnham Castle because his cousin, Charles, remained in residence there until his death in 1874, a year after Wilberforce was killed when out hunting.

Wilberforce was succeeded by Edward Harold Browne (1873-90), a man who liked Farnham very much, and he was followed to

43 Soldiers helped bring a mild prosperity to the people of Hale, some of whom, like Billy Ayres, became hawkers to the troops, taking goods round to them at their huts on the common, and selling from carts. Billy was born in 1881 and married Rose Vinden, at Hale, on 31 March 1902. He died in 1949.

44   When this photograph was taken in 1909, the building which dominates the scene was Farnham Police Station, where Superintendent Simmonds was in charge. Later it was used as a court house but early in 1999 it was advertised as being for sale. The event which has drawn so many people—and choirboys—was the foundation-stone-laying of Church House, Union Road.

the See by Antony Wilson Thorold (1890–5), who was popular in the town. Bishop Randall Davidson (1895–1903), who later became Archbishop of Canterbury, bridged the end of Queen Victoria's reign (1837–1901) and the beginning of that of her eldest son, Edward VII (1901–10). Herbert Ryle (1903–11), was followed by Edward Stuart Talbot (1911–24) then Frank Theodore Woods (1924–32), the

last Bishop of Winchester to be associated with Farnham.

From 1129 to 1932, a period of 803 years, there was a total of 53 Bishops of Winchester, almost all of whom either lived or stayed at Farnham Castle. Trade was generated in the town by visitors staying at either Farnham Castle or Waverley Abbey, and so gradually the town expanded.

Seven

A Time of Change

EVEN THOUGH there is no record of people actually fighting on the streets of Farnham, the Civil War made a difference to the town. The townspeople, on the whole, were for the King (Royalists), but the Round-heads (Parliamentarians) wanted control of Farnham Castle because of the important position it held on the road from London to Winchester, Southampton and many other important towns.

Sir William Waller, the Parliamentarian, captured the castle and made it into his head-quarters for the whole of the south of England. Waller's soldiers were camped in Farnham Park where there was a gallows on which people were hanged for offences such as mutiny. There was also a gallows and stocks at the bottom of Castle Street.

Although I have not been able to find documentary evidence for this word-of-mouth

45 An engraving by F. Evans of Moor Park House in the mid-19th century. Sir William Temple owned the house from 1686-99. Charles Darwin visited Moor Park House when writing *The Origin of the Species*

story, related to me by a nonagenarian in the 1960s, I have checked the building in question and can find no reason to doubt the story. Louisa Budd, who was born in Rowledge in the 1860s, said she had been told by her father, who was told by his father, that there was a signalling post, which enabled military detachments to communicate with each other from West Street to the castle during the period of the Civil War. She said there was a false ceiling to a stable to the rear of the property at 108 (now a charity shop adjacent to the post office), and that a man would lie on his stomach and signal through a grating beneath the eaves. The building was indeed there long before the Civil War began, it had a grating beneath the eaves (although it is now blocked up), and the grating is in a direct line to the castle (although later buildings now obscure the view).

Following a visit by Oliver Cromwell to Farnham Castle, the keep was rendered unfit for further defence, and the people of Farnham used stone and rubble from the damaged building to make road surfaces; even today, if road works go more than a metre below the present tarmac surface in Castle, West and Downing Streets, the limestone from the castle can sometimes be seen.

For the 11 years following the beheading of Charles I in January 1649, there was no monarch. During the period of the Interregnum the townspeople of Farnham prospered even though there were several years when the corn harvest was poor. Messrs. Hall and Gretton, in *Farnham During the Civil Wars and Interregnum 1642-1660*, state that, although hard evidence is lacking about business during this time, they believe it was the period when financial foundations were laid for those who were to become the wealthy merchants and traders of the 18th century, particularly for those who became involved with hop growing. Many of the present buildings in Farnham were already in existence by this time, but most, if not all, have been re-fronted and altered over the past three-and-a-half centuries. The exception is the row

46 The backwaters of the town can often be surprising. Tucked behind Argos, where *Fishing News* was published, a large iron fish was used as an advertisement. To make certain that the lady who cleaned the offices had dusted all the overhead beams each day, management left two pence pieces in different places every night, each of which had to be returned.

of Windsor Almshouses, in Castle Street, which appears from old prints not to have altered at all on the outside although work in the late 1980s changed them internally. What did the eight 'poor, honest, old, impotent' people who lived in them during the Civil War make of the thousands of soldiers in colourful uniforms who invaded the quiet streets of the town? It is quite possible the military personnel were disliked, and maybe it is this deep-seated animosity which is still apparent today amongst the people of Farnham, who tend only to accept officers from the military town of Aldershot, members of the ranks scarcely ever coming here.

Once the monarchy was restored, Bishop Morley used a great deal of money on improving, as well as repairing, the castle. It was he who was responsible for the appearance of the Great Hall as we see it today, with its minstrels' gallery and huge stone fireplace. This was also the time when Isaac Walton, author of *The Compleat Angler*, described the River Wey as having 'the best fish'. Walton was a steward at the castle.

47   The local 'great' in the Great Hall of the town's greatest building. Former M.P. Godfrey Nicholson stands next to present M.P. Virginia Bottomley, while both watch former Farnham School of Art head, James Hockey, cut the 40th anniversary cake of the Farnham Society. Mayors Leslie Fenn and Ken Gosling plus the Society's president, Michael Blower, are also pictured.

Although some of the large houses on the outskirts of town were in existence for most of the 17th century, after the monarchy was restored some of them were upgraded, such as that bought by Sir William Temple, in 1690, Moor Park House. It was here that Jonathan Swift, the author most famous for *Gulliver's Travels*, was employed as secretary to Sir William.

By the end of the 17th century Farnham's position as an important market for wheat was declining. Hops, the small green bracts used to give beer its bitter taste, which had been introduced to the area in 1597 by a Mr. Bignell from Suffolk, were rapidly taking over almost every field around the town, with the hop gardens in which they were grown reaching to the back gardens of the town residents' houses.

Although there are no hop gardens in Farnham today, there are still thousands of residents who can remember hop-picking, two weeks out of school helping mother to pick the bracts which were put into baskets and then checked by a tallyman. At the end of picking, in a good hop year, there might be enough money raised to buy a pair of boots for each child for the winter, and perhaps some clothes, too. A bad year was disastrous for the entire family. Hop-picking also brought visitors to town. Poor people from London would travel on the train, be met at the station by farmers with carts, taken to barns at local farms, and men, women and children would spend the next fortnight sleeping on straw-filled pockets (sacks) at night and working in the fields all day. This was looked upon as an annual holiday.

48 Moor Park House, home of Sir William Temple. Jonathan Swift, the satirist and author of *Gulliver's Travels*, *Tale of a Tub* and many other books, worked for a time as Sir William's secretary.

49 At hop-picking time everyone helped—even small children. Peter Towns, from Middle Church Lane, can be seen here in the hop basket, although usually, to avoid a clip round the ear, children kept well clear of this container. A knock would cause the hops to settle and more would have to be picked before it was deemed full by the tallyman.

50 Farnham Maltings, 1975, seven years after it had been saved from demolition through its purchase by a group of Farnham people, including Dr. A. Crowe, chairman of the Farnham Society, Sir John Verney, artist, Raymond Krish, solicitor, and Lt. Col. Morgan Bransby-Williams, local councillor. Here it looks more like a prison than the community and arts centre which it is today.

51 Hops bines were trained up both single poles and strings. This 19th-century picture shows mothers and children picking the bracts. They would later be dried in the kilns seen in the background, before being packed into pockets (large sacks). This hop garden is believed to have been at Pitt Farm, Frensham. The pockets would later be sold at a hop fair.

Hop bines had to be trained up poles or wires and held in position with ties. The ties were often made from the rushes which grew in a number of places (including the area now known as Hale Reeds, at Heath End), and even small children would help tread the rushes on flagstone floors to make them pliable enough to tie the bines. One of the murals on Farnham Police Station shows men on stilts tying hops. Because men were paid piece rates it was beneficial to use stilts, rather than keep moving a platform along, to reach the tops of the poles, which were about twelve feet from the ground.

Hops grew everywhere and hop kilns were constructed where they could be dried. Evidence of many of these can still be found, for example adjacent to Hone's, Downing Street, as part of the wine cellars of the Lion Brewery Store, West Street, and as part of an office block at the bottom of Crondall Lane.

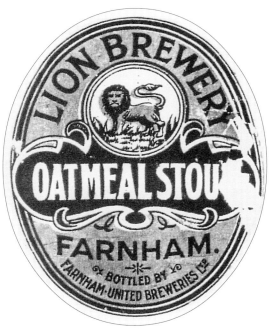

52 A somewhat damaged label off a bottle of Oatmeal Stout from the Lion Brewery, West Street. This was bottled by Farnham United Breweries Ltd., in the early years of the 20th century, before F.U.B. was taken over by Courage and Co.

Maltings were built, so that barley could be steeped until it sprouted, then dried and finally crushed. Farnham Maltings, in Bridge Square, now the second most important venue for Beerex events in this country, is famous among the real ale fraternity nationally, yet few appreciate its original connection with their favourite tipple.

With barley and hops on hand, breweries too were built, the numerous small firms, such as Barlings and Barretts, later amalgamating to form Farnham United Breweries, which was eventually taken over by brewery giant Courage and Company in the 1920s. In 1890 there were at least fifty public houses in the town.

More hops were grown here than could possibly be used locally, however, so they were taken to Weyhill near Andover by 10 October each year, for sale to brewers, particularly those from the West Country, who appreciated the subtle flavour which Farnham hops gave to the beer they produced. At Weyhill Fair, the Farnham hop-planters who were selling their produce had a special section of the market to themselves known as Blissimore Hall Acre; they traded under the name of the Gentlemen of Farnham.

A number of wealthy men decided to go into banking as well. The most famous of these banks was Knight's, which was situated in Castle Street. It later became the Capital and Counties Bank. Lloyds Bank occupies Knight's original site, but not the building. This was demolished in the 1930s because it was considered to be out of keeping with the surrounding architecture.

As people became richer they acquired more personal possessions, such as guns and watches, so more and more gunsmiths and clockmakers set up shop in town, and drapers and outfitters also became more numerous. Greater wealth meant larger houses, which entailed more housework, so staff were employed in this capacity. Young local girls were often able to remain in Farnham to work

53 The Lion Brewery, West Street, preserved in name as Lion Brewery Stores. The buildings which house the off–licence's wine cellars were once part of the brewery, all other parts of which, including a deep well from which the water was obtained, are now beneath a modern housing and office complex. This photograph is from a *Mates Guide*, *c.*1903.

54 A picture of Farnham mothers taking to the bottle might shock many people until they realise that only 'Adam's ale' is being drunk from the empty cod liver oil bottles which had been distributed at Wrecclesham Infant Welfare Clinic almost fifty years ago. Two of the imbibers, at what was, in reality, a party game, were Kath Riddles and Mrs. Freer.

55 Castle Street, *c*.1890, with the Capital and Counties Bank, designed by Norman Shaw, dominating the scene. Earlier this was known as Knights' Bank, the Knights having bought out John Stevens' Bank. Despite its having been copied several times, the name of Rogers on the baker's in The Borough can still be read on this century-old John Henry Knight photograph.

56 One of the lesser-known family names of clock and watchmakers in Farnham is James—Edward and William. Edward was born in 1799, worked until 1874, died in 1893 and is buried in Farnham cemetery. He operated from West Street and Downing Street and his son had premises in The Borough. The clock behind this face still ticks away in Aldershot.

57 Farnham railway station in the Edwardian era, showing the contrasts in male attire at that time. Ned Trusler, from The Bourne, is the man wearing a smock in the centre. The names of the other people are not known. It is believed the occasion is connected with hops—several men have them as buttonholes.

58 In 1959 Sid Riddles shows his baby daughter, Denise, the latest device in the war to keep Farnham tidy. The vehicle, with brushes to sweep the streets, is parked in Weydon Lane, before Pilgrim's Way School was built adjacent to the building behind them. What appears to be a hand-written slogan over the cab window reads, 'Stick to your litter.'

as housemaids rather than go farther afield. More food was required, and many more grocery shops, butchers, fishmongers and bakers were opened.

Some of the Georgian houses of note include Willmer House (now the Museum of Farnham), Sandford House and Bethune House (all in West Street), and Ivy House (now the Conservative Club, off Downing Street). When building a complete house was more than a businessman could afford with ease, the front of an older building could be 'Georgianized'. Thus many which appear to have been constructed in the Georgian period, such as a number in Castle Street, are seen to be much older once one steps inside the front door.

National Fire Laws had been introduced, so it was decided in 1754 that Farnham should have its own fire engine, a wonderful wooden construction, with bars at both sides which were moved up and down to pump the water. The engine, which has been repaired and preserved, is now at the Surrey Fire Brigade headquarters in Reigate.

Several nonconformist chapels were opened, including one which had its own burial ground in front of it. This was on the site of the present Swain and Jones garage and show-room on the north side of East Street. On 22 December 1989 a mass re-burial took place in the West Street cemetery after the remains of 29 bodies had been found during work at the garage. A decade earlier a few other bodies had been found at the same site. These too were re-interred soon after they were discovered.

Straddling the 18th and 19th centuries is Farnham's most famous son, William Cobbett. He was born in Bridge Square, at what is now known as the *William Cobbett* public house, in 1763, and died at Normandy Farm, Ash, in 1835. He is buried close to the main door of St Andrew's Church. He was known as 'The Poor Man's Friend' because he never forgot his own humble beginnings. He had no formal education yet taught himself to read

and write, was responsible for founding *Cobbett's Political Register* as well as *Political Debates*, which became known as *Hansard*, the record of everything which is said in both the House of Commons and House of Lords, wrote many books and articles, including the international classic *Rural Rides*, and became, towards the end of his life, a member of parliament. There are many biographical works about Cobbett and a society is devoted to the great man.

At the time of Cobbett's birth, those people who were too old or too sick to fare for themselves were put into the workhouse in Middle Church Lane, a place which had filled this role since 1726. It is still in existence and can be identified by the building with a letterbox in the centre of a wall rather than a door. The residents who were forced to go there looked out from its windows on to their next and final 'home'—the graveyard.

By the time Cobbett was 27 years old, in 1790, a new workhouse was built just outside the town area, at what was eventually called Hale Road. It was later to be known as St Andrew's Homes. It remained there for about 180 years (although at the end of the 19th century Farnham Workhouse was described as 'a reproach to England', so bad were the conditions), before being demolished to make way for a hospital laundry. This has also now been demolished and the site is vacant, soon to be covered with private houses if the nearby former site of St James's Homes is any indication. This complex, completed in 1939 to very high specifications and mainly on one floor, was demolished, almost overnight, and in 1997 a Barrett Homes complex sprang up almost as quickly.

Like William Cobbett, 'the Poor Man's Friend', Florence Nightingale, 'the lady with the lamp', was also much loved by ordinary men and women, particularly the soldiers to whom she ministered as a nurse during the Crimean War.

59 Two boys with 34 girls—no wonder Frank Wibaut, on the left, looks somewhat bemused. The young lad on the right is staring into space as he stands amongst this line-up of short-socked young ladies in the Farnham Children's Choir, posing for the photographer in the United Reformed Church Hall in the mid-1950s. Frank later became a concert pianist.

60 William Cobbett (1763-1835), arguably Farnham's most famous person, was the third son of a man who was both a farmer and innkeeper. William has been described as 'one of the most remarkable self-taught men of whom England can boast'. His most famous work is *Rural Rides* and he was also the founder of *Cobbett's Political Debates* which later became *Hansard*.

61 *The Jolly Farmer*, Bridge Square, birthplace of the great William Cobbett, in 1763, and known today as the *William Cobbett*. The shop and house on the right of this picture are now also part of the inn. This is one of the most photographed buildings in Farnham although few pictures show, as this does, the words Wine and Spirit Merchant on the fascia board.

62 Major Ken Hocking and Mrs. Elfrida Manning, two of Farnham's notables, lay a wreath at William Cobbett's tomb in St Andrew's Church-yard, just outside the main church door, in the mid–1980s. William was born in Farnham and spent his childhood in the town. He died at Normandy Farm, near Ash, about five miles from his birthplace, in 1835.

Florence was not a native of Farnham but was a frequent visitor to the town, where she stayed with the Paget family at Lowlands (later Brightwell House and more recently part of the Redgrave Theatre). Miss Nightingale gave a silver communion set to Farnham Hospital, to be used by ministers visiting the hospital to give communion to the sick and dying. Another visitor to the Paget household was Arthur, later Sir Arthur, Sullivan, one half of the Gilbert and Sullivan partnership. Sir Arthur wrote a piece of music entitled *Farnham Idyll*, which he sent to the Pagets following a visit to the town at hop-picking time, when the air was filled with the pungent odour of hops.

63 Brightwell House, earlier known as Lowlands, in 1950, when it was the home of the Paget family. Both Florence Nightingale and Arthur Sullivan were regular visitors here. Latterly it has been a restaurant, part of the Redgrave Theatre, which closed in 1998. It faces a sward which might soon be used for housing in the East Street regeneration plan.

64 Farnham men were given a good send-off, in Castle Street, when they left to join the ranks of soldiers who went to fight for their country in 1914. The cars in the background had brought, amongst others, men of the Surrey Volunteer Reserves, to join others before they marched to Farnham Station.

65 There were once toll-houses on all the approach roads to Farnham. After road fund licences replaced the toll, the houses were privately occupied. Some, like this one at Runfold photographed in 1924, were used as meeting places for members of the Cyclists' Touring Club—its swinging sign can be seen fixed to the wall.

66 Brigadier General Sir Edward Perceval lived at The Grange, Castle Street. He was one of the first customers to open an account at the Midland Bank, Farnham, in 1921, when Mr. Lewis was manager. This drawing of Castle Street, made in 1926 and another of the Rose Garden at The Grange, were later given by Sir Edward to Mr. Lewis.

The Bishop of Winchester had given Farnham people its borough, a gift of freedom, but it had never been a royal borough with a mayor. By 1789 there was only one person left who was prepared to be a bailiff, and when he found that he was paying out of his own pocket for the upkeep of things like bridges, even he decided to call it a day. He returned all the town's records to the Bishop of Winchester and it became a place, like most others, ruled by a parish government.

As more and more horse-drawn traffic came through the town it was deemed prudent to set up turnpikes, whereby a fee had to be paid to help with the repair and maintenance of the rough roads. There was a toll-gate near Bourne Mill in the east, near Willey Mill in the west, just south of The Grange, in Castle Street, to the north and, until 1790, when it was demolished to help with the flow of traffic, at the top of Downing Street.

Eight

Nuisances and Novelties

IMPORTANT AS IT HAS ALWAYS considered itself, in the census for 1801 the Farnham population numbered just 321. A century later it had risen more than fourteen-fold, and by the year 2001 around 36,000 names would appear on the census for this town.

When Queen Victoria ascended the throne Farnham was, therefore, a small but prosperous town three miles from the tiny village of Aldershot. Law and order was maintained by a town constable and a couple of nightwatchmen. A police station was opened in Bear Lane in the middle of the century and was later transferred to Union Road, where the much-loved Superintendent Simmonds lived on site with his large family. The nightwatchmen who patrolled the streets also shouted out the time. Only horse-drawn

67 There are police as far as the eye can see for the funeral in 1926 of former Superintendent Arthur Simmonds, of Normandie, Firgrove Hill. While he was in office, and recovering from being thrown by a horse, the townspeople paid to have straw placed outside his home in Union Road, so that the noise of horses' hooves would not disturb him.

coaches were available to transport people between Farnham and the metropolis; the River Wey frequently burst its banks; the major industry was hops, growing, harvesting or using them in brewing. The large Georgian, and earlier, houses occupied prime sites in West Street and Castle Street, and the poor lived in tiny cottages hidden away in small courtyards, probably to stop them spoiling the grand streets which were occupied by the wealthy.

The coming of the South Western Railway line from London in 1848/9 changed the horizons of everyone in Farnham. It was well used, especially after the military camp was opened at Aldershot, which was without a station. Until then it is unlikely that many residents had ever been to London and even fewer would have seen the sea, in spite of both being less than 35 miles away in different directions. At a cost of 2s. 11d., a third-class journey could be taken to London, the rate charged at just one penny per mile, even less for a return ticket. However, the railway brought problems, too. It was proposed that a road be built linking Castle Street directly with the station but one person would not sell his land, so New Road (now known as South Street) was constructed, from the East Street/Bear Lane/Borough junction. It went through the former town cricket ground, so cricket went back to Farnham Park, where it has remained to this day.

Then the level crossing, which allowed trains to cross over the Tilford Road/Waverley Lane/Station Road junction caused arguments. The proposed solution was the construction of a detour for traffic through The Fairfield, over a new bridge about 150 yards to the east of the level crossing, and through Broomleaf Farm, to rejoin the road close to the *Waverley Arms*.

The closest the town ever came to having this scheme implemented was in 1896. At that time Mr. Samuel Bircham from the railway company wanted the council to take the railway's surface water into the town's drainage system. If the council would agree to this and

68 In the mid-1950s Farnham's Victorian railway station was still lit by gas lamps. Milk from local farms was transported by churn and train up the line to London. This drawing by Terence Blackwell, a former Farnham Grammar School pupil and student at Farnham School of Art, was made when he was carrying out National Service in the R.A.F.

to keep the road over the Firgrove railway bridge in good repair, the railway company would give the town a strip of land near the level crossing for road widening and pay £50 (later raised to £70) as well. At a special meeting of the council on 9 November 1896, the subject was fully discussed and the fact that 200 people objected to the idea was noted. The matter remained on the agenda into the new year and the project was even written into the London & South Western Railway Company (Various Powers) Bill, which was with Parliament, a deadline for objections being set for 16 February 1897. On 8 February Farnham Council members decided they would remain neutral over the matter and the fight would be between the town's taxpayers and the railway authorities.

More ratepayers objected to the railway proposals, and on 9 March 1897 Mr. Bircham attended a special meeting of the council to tell them that because around 400 ratepayers now objected to the proposal the railway company was withdrawing its offer of money and land. In future those people who were held up at the gates would have to blame not the railway but former Farnham residents for the delay they experienced.

The railway was popular with businessmen who could work in London and return to a home in Farnham at night. Land was cheaper to the south of the town and so areas such as the Ridgeway and the Bourne began to have modern Victorian houses built there. George Sturt vividly recalls the influence of such houses and people on the residents of the Bourne in his book *Change in the Village*.

Gravel was used again for roads and railway tracks. Many gravel and sand pits were opened on the outskirts of town and, later, often filled in with household refuse. At the end of the 20th century there is still controversy over the winnowing of gravel, particularly at Runfold and Coxbridge.

The old Market House was demolished in 1866 and the first of Farnham's two Town Halls (which was called the Corn Exchange) was built at the bottom of Castle Street. This was replaced about sixty years later by the present building, which has a model of the *Golden Hind*, covered in gold leaf, above its tower. In 1986 local architect Max Lyons, who

69 The Borough about a century ago, a view which shows that the only real change in buildings is the replacement of the old Corn Exchange/Town Hall at the corner of Castle Street. The lady in white stands outside the *Goat's Head*, at number 40, John Nichols, printer, is at 41, Sturt's booksellers at 42, the Misses Williamson, stationers, at 43, and Holden's shoe shop at 44.

70 The only surviving building in this view, down Bear Lane, towards the East Street/Borough/South Street junction, is that bearing chimney pots, now part of a building society. All the others have been sacrificed to the requirements of horse-power or offices. St Polycarp's Church, left, was replaced by St Joan of Arc's in Tilford Road in the 1930s.

was responsible for the building of the upper part of Lion and Lamb Yard, put a second golden ship aloft, on a building at the top of the yard. This was a copy of the *Mary Rose*, Henry VIII's flagship.

More people were having their children (or at least their sons) educated, and the chantry chapel, where boys had been taught and the forerunner of Farnham Grammar School, was soon too small. A new school was built in West Street in 1872, and it has remained a place of education ever since. Education has always played a big part in the life of Farnham town, from the days when boys were taught in a room at the side of the parish church, through to the present, when South Farnham School (formerly Farnham Girls' Grammar School) achieved joint first position, in Surrey, in

Government league tables published in February 1999. Adult and art education has also been an important feature of town life. At the end of the 19th century there were reading rooms for men at the Grammar School in West Street and at the Working Men's Institute which was held in the Freemason's Hall at the top of Castle Street. Here, too, boys from local schools went to learn woodwork and their sisters were taught cookery and laundry skills. W.H. Allen was the first head of Farnham School of Art, which began in The Borough in 1865 and moved to 17 South Street in 1870.

In 1890 the first Catholic church in Farnham for more than 400 years was built in Bear Lane, adjacent to Catholic St Polycarp's School and the police station. The congregation soon outgrew this church and a new one, dedicated to St Joan of Arc, was built in Tilford Road in the 1930s. Farnham had been hospitable to Catholic priests fleeing France at the time of the Revolution, and between 1797 and 1802 it is believed that more than 200 lived in this town (a number equal to more than two-thirds of the indigenous population according to the 1801 census). One cleric is on record as saying: 'This town is rich and its inhabitants are very generous towards the exiled priests.'

The town might have been considered rich, but clean water was still a luxury. There was a conduit near Farnham Castle and another at the bottom of Castle Street, just under the present arcade and marked by a small piece of metal in a flagstone. Water was taken from door to door and sold at 1d. a bucket.

Drainage (or rather lack of it) caused problems in Farnham throughout the Victorian era, and it was not until the mid-1880s that sewers were laid in town—in one enormous operation. Prior to that, during the hours of darkness night-soil men went around emptying cesspits and taking the contents to a place just beyond the town limit—Mount Pleasant—the name given to many places where human refuse was dumped (including that of the City of London, where the head post office is today)!

A Local Board for the Urban District was formed in 1866 and in 1894 Farnham Urban District Council was created. This survived until it was taken over by Waverley Borough Council in 1974, much to the displeasure of many residents who thought they were being treated as the poor relations of the larger body. During the period from December 1884 to June 1886, £14,000 went into the Local Government Board's coffers, paid into Knight's

71 St Joan of Arc Church, Tilford Road. Father Robo, its French founder, is said to have insisted it should be built facing Farnham Castle because the latter was home of the Bishops of Winchester, who, he said, were responsible for the death of St Joan. He wanted to give them a constant reminder of this in the form of his church.

Bank by the Loans Board, in bi-monthly instalments of £1,500. In *Victorian Farnham*, Bill Ewbank Smith cites a number of examples of members of the local hierarchy receiving perks from the fund, including a rise in salary for the Clerk of the Council, giving him £100 per annum, and an award to the Surveyor of an additional £20 per annum. Mr. Ewbank Smith adds: 'Whilst charity had not actually begun at home, what was left had now arrived on home ground.'

Most householders still had to fetch water from a nearby pump or well, none being laid on in the artisans' cottages, and this water was often contaminated. Overcrowding was common, wages were low and often irregular, medical attention had to be paid for, and there were no antibiotics, so illnesses and infections normally had to run their course. During epidemics of measles, diphtheria and scarlet fever schools were closed to try to contain the outbreaks. Children who did not arrive at school in a clean and tidy condition, or had head lice, were usually sent home.

Doctors Sloman, father and son, appear to have done their best for the poorer people in the town with regard to both their water supply and sanitary arrangements, and in 1892 Dr. Sloman junior gave a grave warning about the serious risk of cholera in Red Lion Lane because of polluted water from the shallow wells. Samples tested by the county analyst were found to be sewage-polluted and dangerous, quite unfit for drinking purposes, and his report eventually led to a water main being laid along that street.

It was not just in private homes that the drains caused problems. Even in one of the newly-built schools in West Street, the boys' latrines were in question. West Street Board School had been opened in 1896 with accommodation for 270 boys in four rooms, the largest of which, intended for 120 boys, measured 60 feet in length and 22 feet in width. Mr. John Lewis was the headmaster and for three-and-a-half years he worried about the

The . .
Farnham Sanitary Laundry Co. Ltd.

Telephone : 107

Largest and Best Laundry - - in the District - -

SNOW-WHITE :: LINEN

:: PURE WATER ::
FROM OUR OWN ARTESIAN WELLS
*
LARGE OPEN-AIR DRYING GROUNDS

Special Terms for Customers sending Linen per Rail.

No Chemicals used. Work executed by Hand or Power, as desired.
Trial Solicited. Inspection of Premises Invited.
— PRICE LIST ON APPLICATION —

72 The Farnham Sanitary Laundry, largest and best in the district, advertised that it used pure water from its own artesian wells, had large, open-air drying grounds, worked by hand or power, as desired, and a trial was solicited and inspection of the premises invited. Customers sending linen to the laundry by rail were given a special discount.

toilets. On 16 June 1896 he wrote in the school log book,

the water supply for sanitary arrangements is a failure—no flush has been through the latrines, from the cistern, for some time. The cleansing is now done by the caretaker, with a bucket, which is insufficient.

In June 1899, after a surveyor's report and another from the medical officer, the matter was rectified in just two days!

73 When new paving was being laid in the Town Hall Arcade, a local woman noted that the stone in the foreground with a small piece of metal handle remaining, which marked the Victorian conduit supplying fresh water to the town's residents, was to be removed. Determined it should remain, she harangued the works foreman who gave in and worked round it.

74 Architect Harold Falkner's arch remains as an entrance to the Victoria Garden, but the wall in the background, which shielded bathers for more than seventy-five years at Farnham's open-air swimming pool, has now been replaced by sheltered accommodation. Brightwell's Tennis Courts, in the foreground, will also disappear soon if the East Street regeneration takes place as planned.

75 Sir Ray Tindle was born on 8 October 1926 and educated at Torquay Grammar and Strand School. Today he is proprietor of almost 100 newspaper titles, including the *Farnham Herald* and *Surrey and Hants News*, plus several radio stations. He lives and works in Farnham. His media empire was built up from the small post-war gratuity he received after serving in the Devonshire Regiment, 1944-7.

After the open-air swimming baths, built to commemorate Queen Victoria's Diamond Jubilee in 1897, were provided by public subscription, boys from West Street Board School were allowed to use the pool on Fridays from 1.30 p.m. to 3.30 p.m., under the supervision of their masters, as long as they brought their own bathing drawers and towels. Children from other schools used the baths at other specified times and they were open to all during the evenings, Saturdays and holiday times. The only part of these baths which remains is a wall and arch, designed by Harold Falkner, situated behind the Liberal Club, South Street, the latter being Edwin Lutyens' first public building.

A gasworks opened in East Street in 1834 and was only demolished about 135 years later. It is still not possible to build homes on the land because the earth is contaminated by the gas.

The *Surrey and Hants News* was printed and published by Mr. W. Lucy from his establishment at 1, The Borough, from 1859. In 1892 Mr. Ernest Langham started a newspaper in South Street, the *Weekly Herald*, which soon became the *Farnham Herald*, so Mr. Lucy had competition. Now under the same owner, Sir Ray Tindle, both newspapers (and their sister papers covering Haslemere, Bordon, Petersfield and Alton) are still printed and published in this town.

One of Farnham's rare demonstrations of working men's power, widely reported in the local newspapers, took place early in 1897. Sir William Rose, Bart. had bought Moor Park House in 1890 but did not like the townsfolk crossing it on a public footpath because (he said) they sometimes peered into his property. The path which they trod, down the side of the *Shepherd and Flock* in Guildford Road, led to Mother Ludlam's Cave, a local attraction and an ideal place for a Sunday afternoon stroll. He had complained intermittently for seven years, and on 4 January 1897 his solicitors wrote and told the council that their client intended to close the lodge gates at Moor Park and not allow any person to enter without written authority.

The council replied that they had no doubt as to the rights of way over Moor Park and were resolved, at whatever cost, to use all proper means to preserve such rights. At a special meeting on 15 January a message was read stating that Sir William still intended to close the gates and this would occur two days later. The Urban District Council ordered that Mr. Herbert Frost, its surveyor, should be present on the Sunday and should take some workmen with him, and that 'if any obstructions to the right-of-way be found, that he [Mr. Frost] do remove same.'

On a cold and snowy Sunday morning, 17 January 1897, Sir William's men, including a number of ex-Metropolitan Police that he had hired, closed and chained the gates. A crowd of around 500 townsfolk, mostly men (the women no doubt at home cooking the Sunday lunch), gathered at the site. Mr. Frost and a colleague, John Stedman, forced the chains with crowbars, the crowd, armed with crowbars, sledge hammers, sticks and even snowballs, cheered and pushed their way into Moor Park. The defenders, a few lodgekeepers and servants plus the six ex-policemen, were no match for a tenth of the town's population, so the working men won a victory which has never since been challenged.

By the end of Victoria's reign, in 1901, Farnham was an even more prosperous town of around 5,000 inhabitants, with a main line railway to London, two grammar schools and an art school, high class shops, plenty of work for servants in houses occupied by officers from the military camp at Aldershot, and what was said to be the highest concentration of public houses per head of population of any town in the country. Producing hops was still the way to make most money in the area.

Nine

Yards and Yards in Farnham

THE WORD 'YARD', as defined by the *Oxford English Dictionary*, comes from the Old English *geard*, meaning a fence, dwelling or house, and adds that the Old English for an orchard is *ortgeard*. A yard is a comparatively small, uncultivated area attached to a building or enclosed by it, especially such an area surrounded by walls or buildings within the precincts of a castle, house, inn, etc., i.e. backyard, stableyard, innyard, and by 1808 the word had also come to mean a school playground. The dictionary further notes that a yard was a place where cattle or poultry were kept, and was also an enclosure devoted to some work or business, such as a brickyard. With such a wide range of possibilities, most towns in the past had many 'yards' leading off the main streets, but Farnham is possibly unique in retaining such a large number at the end of the 20th century.

At the highest point of the town centre is the courtyard at Farnham Castle, a place now seen by hundreds of people each year. The castle is now the Centre for International Briefing but for more than 800 years it was the home of the Bishops of Winchester, and the many monarchs who walked in it must have noted the sun glinting in the stained glass windows and, looking upwards to the sky, felt a sense of both piety and security in this ecclesiastical fortress.

For those who walk down from the castle—traversing seven steps then counting seven strides on a flat area, followed by another seven steps and another seven strides until the pathway is reached—there are a number of further yards to see in Castle Street. Close to the *Nelson Arms*, through the central gate in the block of 17th-century almshouses, and beyond the length of the wall of the cottages, can be seen a delightful communal courtyard which was far larger than at present until more dwellings for elderly people were constructed there in the late 1980s, at about the time the aforementioned eight cottages were made into four homes.

A few steps farther down the street, on the same side as the almshouses, is the courtyard in front of a pizza restaurant. From 1939 to 1974 the Castle Theatre was situated here. This was the forerunner of the Redgrave Theatre. The building dates from the 16th century and is reputed to have been a barn where servants at the castle slept. Over the years it has been a wagon shed, store house, roller-skating rink, cinema, de-lousing station for First World War soldiers, the manufactory for Quinettes soft drinks (bought out by Kia Ora in the 1930s), as well as a theatre of which Sir Michael Redgrave said, 'It is the most haunted theatre in which I have ever played.' It has been a restaurant for at least twenty years.

Almost adjacent to this courtyard is the playground of the former St George's School. The house in which children were taught is now a private residence, and the former playground is a garden area, but until comparatively recently the sound of children's voices at play could regularly be heard drifting over the rooftops and into the street.

76 Courage Alton Ales are on sale in the *Nelson Arms* and there is a post-box in the wall. Apart from these differences, this 1945 picture of the Windsor Almshouses shows them as they must have looked when they were built over three hundred years ago.

77 Gerald Flood (possibly most famous as Inspector Mahmoud in the television series *The Rat Catchers*), and his wife Ann, celebrated their wedding reception in the haunted foyer of the former Castle Theatre, 1949. In its 400-year-history this building has housed servants from Farnham Castle, been a skating rink, silent cinema, Quinettes soft drinks firm and a restaurant.

Just two doors away from the former school is the entrance to what is now known as St Georges Yard. Despite criticism from local journalists and teachers of English grammar, the developer of St Georges Yard insisted that no apostrophe should be used in the name. This courtyard has had a chequered history too, having in recent years enclosed an auction house, a postal sorting office and a carpet warehouse. In the past it was the site of a pub, originally known as *The Lamb*, which in the 18th century changed its name to the *Lamb and Flag* and later still to the *Bell and Crown*. A small factory making hop pockets (sacks) was established behind the *Bell and Crown* in the 1820s. Following closure by the licensing authorities in 1902, the pub was demolished in 1910 and for many years the yard was the Watney, Combe and Reid brewery depot. Two of this brewery's principals lived locally, Mr. Combe at Pierrepont, Frensham, and Mr. Reid at the *Shepherd and Flock* on the Guildford Road. In the 1980s a market selling fish, fruit, vegetables and clothing operated from here but its attraction soon waned and the fishmonger, with his barrow from London's Billingsgate Market, moved into Castle Street while the other stallholders packed up and left.

78 The motor car had arrived in Castle Street by the early 1950s. The building on the extreme left is part of the former St George's School, and the bar stretching between two buildings, on which the Royal Coat of Arms and the words Watney, Combe, Reid & Co. Ltd. are written, now carries the words 'St Georges Yard'.

79 In 1896 James Riddles founded a nursery business at The Conifers, Rowledge. He moved to Green Lane, Shortheath, in 1908, and his son, Frank, later carried on the firm. Frank can be seen in the cab of the nursery's van at a time when they were known as market gardeners. Fruit and vegetables could be purchased from a wooden shed on the site.

The metal waterhead on a nearby building contains the entwined initials of HWB, standing for H.W. Bodkin, a tailor who operated from a shop here for many years. Behind the shop was a yard where his grandchildren used to play. It is believed that in the late 19th century, rooms above the adjacent shop were used as a home for unmarried pregnant girls who were allowed to stay here until after their confinement.

Within a few feet the old *Goat's Head* inn yard was situated. This hostelry was at the bottom of Castle Street, with the old Market House, dating from 1568, outside its main entrance. Both the Market House and the inn

were demolished in the 1860s when the new Gothic-style bank, designed by Norman Shaw, was built. This was subsequently replaced by the present Lloyds Bank building, designed by Harold Falkner, one of Farnham's most eccentric architects, in the 1930s. A very early photograph shows the *Goat's Head* (which dated from around 1796) before a fire destroyed most of the premises. Remnants of the extensive, older stabling survived, though, along the rear of the units now known as Town Hall Buildings.

The Bailiff's House in The Borough, the building at the extreme right of the present Town Hall arcade, was sympathetically restored by Harold Falkner in the 1930s. Originally it was the back entrance to the *Goat's Head* stables.

On the right-hand side of Castle Street, with the castle behind, are some narrow alley entrances leading to rows of what were once artisans' cottages. The group known as Lowndes Buildings, for example, now desirable town centre properties, was once nicknamed 'Rabbit Villas' on account of the large number of children in each family who somehow managed to exist in the two-up, two-down cottages, with a privy in the tiny backyard of each.

A slightly wider entrance leads to the Long Garden Walk cottages, on the Castle Street end of the first of which can still be seen a painted advertisement for Tily, an ironmonger's business which operated from a premises close by. Iron grates and stoves are also advertised on the painted advertisement which covers the whole of the top floor and roofline area of the cottage. The 'walk' was where rope was twisted, and comb-like devices stretched down both sides of the path to keep the rope fibres from becoming tangled before twisting took place.

The building in Castle Street which now houses Caffe Uno also has an advertisement painted on the wall above its front door. It pinpoints the site of the ironmonger in question, and behind double gates leading to the former shop's yard, can be found a large garden with

80 Harry Bodkin's tailor's shop, Castle Street, in 1937, when the street was decorated for the coronation of King George VI and Queen Elizabeth. The sign on the lamp-post directs those in need to the 'Public Lavatories' which were once in Park Row but are now offices. What is believed to be an Aldershot and District Traction Company bus is in the foreground.

81 A country spot in the heart of town: young Jim Bodkin and his mother, Emily Olive May Bodkin (neé Mells), are photographed in the garden to the rear of H. Bodkin, at 76 Castle Street, in 1936. The garden is now occupied by extensions both to W.H. Smith, in The Borough, and Lloyds Bank in Castle Street.

Watney Combe Reid & Co. Ltd.
(Close to Capital & Counties Bank)
CASTLE STREET
Telephone :
41 Farnham
FARNHAM, SURREY

ALE & STOUT SUPPLIED IN CASK & BOTTLE

**WINES & SPIRITS OF THE BEST QUALITY
ALWAYS IN STOCK**

Price Lists on Application   -::-   Delivery to all parts

G. E. ALDRIDGE, Manager

82 The name Watney, Combe and Reid can still be seen in Castle Street today, on the bar carrying the words 'St Georges Yard'. The guide book in which this 1920s advertisement is featured also says of the Hog's Back: 'The surface is perfection, the way is solitary.'

a summer house. Before the ironmongery operated from here this was a public house called the *Fleur de Lys* (sometimes the *Fleur de Luce*) and as far back as 1738 it is believed to have been the site of an inn known as the *White Lion* (also *White Lyon*). The horses and carriages of travellers would have been stabled in the yard behind the gates for safety at night.

Hop gardens, also known as hop yards,

stretched from the backs of all the buildings on this side of Castle Street, and in a transaction made in 1738 between John Mayne of Farnham and Henry Mayne of London both the inn and hop gardens adjoining were sold for £600.

Until the 1950s a mural could be seen on an upstairs wall of an adjacent building, which once formed part of the inn. It was believed to have been made by monks who stayed at the inn and who painted the mural in exchange for their board and lodging.

Other yards on this side of the street include those behind a jeweller's and pawn-broker's, and an estate agent's office.

The Borough, at the bottom of Castle Street, forms a cross with the street which for centuries led to the episcopal residence. The Borough, in keeping with Castle Street, West Street, East Street and Downing Street, all have properties which are numbered consecutively as opposed to the more usual evens on one side and odds on the other. Thus The Borough starts at the top of Downing Street and runs through to the Bear Lane/East Street/South Street junction. Being the oldest of the main shopping streets in the town, it at one time had yards behind every property. They were used for slaughtering animals, recreation, making tiles, stabling and even for the manu-facture of corset stays.

The most famous, and still by far the most popular yard, is that behind the great gates at the archway entrance to the *Bush Hotel*. As in many other cases in Farnham, the large *Bush* gates have a smaller entrance within the larger one, for pedestrian use at night once the horses were secured in the courtyard.

The *Bush* is reputed to be the oldest of Farnham's inns and is believed to have existed since at least the 14th century. There is little documentary evidence, however, before the early 17th century, when it was described as 'an ancient inn'. In addition to being an important coaching inn, the *Bush* was the meeting place for special events in the town, such as the Venison Dinner, and at one time

83 The courtyard of the *Bush Hotel* in the 1930s, drawn by Marshall Ward, showing few signs of the vine on the central wall which later gave its name to the bar behind it—before it was modernised in the 1990s, to Bar Tabac. A yard which once housed horse-drawn carts later admitted automobiles; now it's Shanks's Pony only.

The Courtyard, Bush Hotel, Farnham

84 The corner of South Street and The Borough, about 80 years ago. Ransom's the baker's premises (later a bank) was demolished in the 1980s and rebuilt. The sign of a bell, above the letter 'T' in 'caterer', advises customers that a telephone for the use of the public was inside the shop. Mitchell's tobacconist's shop is at the right.

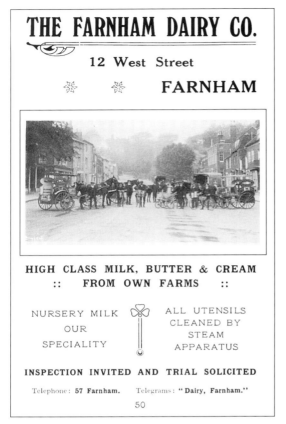

85 This illustration is from an advertisement for the Farnham Dairy, at 12 West Street, featured in *Burrow's Pocket Guide*, *c*.1920. The delivery carts and horses are stretched across Castle Street. Nursery milk was the dairy's speciality and, apparently, 'all utensils were cleaned by steam apparatus. To telephone ring Farnham 57 or send a telegram to Dairy, Farnham.'

86 Charles Borelli, watchmaker and jeweller, sent photographic Christmas cards each year. This view of Borelli Yard, with its archway dated 1610, was taken in the late 1940s. His nephew, later Father Borelli, a Catholic priest, used to play cricket across The Borough, at this point. In this yard, too, Harold Falkner, architect, stored old building materials to re-use.

there were substantial lands attached to the hotel known as Bush Meadows. In addition there were tennis courts, stables and a large garden. The *Bush* courtyard had wooden setts until the mid-1980s and when they were eventually removed to make way for a more durable form of paving, the old oak blocks were burned on the open fires in the hotel bars and lounge. The fountain was constructed at the same time and was for a while a place in which to throw coins and make a wish, as well as an impromptu paddling pool for small children. Keeping the

water clean and fresh caused problems however, so today it is filled with plants.

A short distance westwards is Borelli Yard with its datemark of 1610 firmly fixed to a beam under the archway and behind the large gates which, like the *Bush*, have a smaller gate within one of them. This yard, and the buildings round it, were owned for many years by the Borelli family, who were jewellers, silversmiths and clockmakers and held the Royal Warrant to Queen Victoria. The yard contained domestic buildings and stores and led to a large garden with tennis courts. Many of these buildings, including a large unit where Harold Falkner stored shop-fronts, tiles, bricks and other architectural items which he rescued from premises being demolished (including the famous front at 104a West Street), disappeared under the tarmac of the central car park, offices and the housing complex built by Kents Developments in the mid-1980s. In front of the office units, which have the appearance of town houses round a quadrangle, is a piece of sculpture, 'The Matriarch', by Ben Franklin, one of the town's most eminent sculptors, who taught at the West Surrey College of Art and Design (now the Surrey Institute of Art and Design University College) for 25 years and who died in 1986.

During the development a medieval tile kiln was discovered as well as what was believed to be part of the original town ditch. An iron plaque on a wall in the courtyard shows what the kiln would have looked like. The late Father Borelli, who died in 1997, was a nephew of Charles Borelli. Charles was a friend of Harold Falkner and both men did much to protect the fabric of Farnham. Father Borelli remembered, as a child, playing cricket across The Borough with the stumps situated just under the archway of the yard. He recalled, too, that if a client entered the Borelli shop and wanted an eye test, this had to be carried out in a back room of the building, one which doubled as a dining room for the Borelli family. He remembered being told by his aunt to leave his tea on the table and go into the kitchen while his uncle carried out the examination. The main buildings here are of the early 17th century, with 18th-century and 20th-century additions.

Not now open to the public is the yard which was formerly behind a baker's called Rogers, next door to Borelli's. In the 1920s pickles, chutneys and confectionery were made in the yard at the rear of the premises. Hot toffee was pushed through a machine resembling a mincer, twisted into small pieces and then cut to make humbugs. One young woman

who made the pickles said, when she was in her 90s, that anyone who saw the half-rotten fruit and vegetables that went into the products would have been put off eating it for life. The former baker's premises houses a sports shop today.

Although the name plate of the next yard reads Goat's Head Passage, it actually forms part of Nichol's Yard. This is the name given to the area between the National Westminster Bank and the Bally shoe shop with its spinning wheel sign. John Nichols, born in 1796, bought the premises which the shoe shop now occupies, in 1827, and started a post office in it. In 1839 the Royal Mail coach called there

87 This superb shop-front with putty-moulded decoration, was *in situ* in The Cornhill, London, 200 years ago. It now fronts an employment agency, although for around forty years it was the office of the *Surrey and Hants News*, Surrey's oldest newspaper. The shop-front was brought to Farnham by Harold Falkner. Its twin is in the Victoria and Albert Museum.

88 Hone's greengrocery business was started in 1917, by the grandfather of the present owner, Jonathan Durham. Although Grandfather Hone and his wife had 11 children, their daughter, Dorothy, left, with sister Mabel, said that her father started the shop to 'give her mother something to do'. The shop remains traditional, with fresh produce window displays and goods sold by the pound.

at 3.15 a.m. each day. In 1865 the Nichols family sold the premises and it became a beerhouse known as the *Goat's Head*. It took this name, and the licence, from the original beerhouse of the same name in Castle Street, which had been demolished in the 1860s following a fire.

A brown wooden door, close to the entrance to a dentist's surgery and adjacent to an estate agent, leads into the Farnham bee-keepers' garden and a paved area which was, until a few years ago, still part of the yard

behind the Conservative Club, the front door of which is off Downing Street. During building work for an extension to Boots, a number of interesting finds were made, including a large circular stone where baleen was turned to make stays for corsets. Better known as whalebone, baleen is the elastic, horny substance which grows in a series of thin, parallel plates in the upper jaw of certain whales in place of teeth. Ivy House, built about 1700, has been the Farnham Conservative Club since 1887, but was a corset factory for 32 years before its political affiliation. Aluminium and bristle toothbrushes were produced at the nearby Al Arak toothbrush manufactory.

Almost facing the 'beekeepers' yard', on the other side of The Borough, lies Old Kiln Yard, tucked down the side of Woolworths. In the 1930s it was a photographic studio run by Evelyn (but always known as Jo) Simmonds, one of the daughters of the town's senior police officer, Superintendent A. Simmonds. Jo's story is a sad one. Before the First World War she was one of Farnham's first female photographers and worked for Eugene Fuller at his Delaunay Studio in West Street. When the war was at its height, Mr.

Fuller started to receive white feathers, suggesting he was a coward for not enlisting. He decided to join the army and left Jo in charge of the studio. Unfortunately he was blinded so was no longer able to carry on his profession. Jo continued to run it for him until 1931 when, after an engagement to John Wells, whose parents owned Wells' Bookshop in Castle Street, she sold the photography business, a few weeks before her expected wedding day. In those days women were not expected to work after marriage. Three weeks before the ceremony, however, John Wells was killed in a motorcycle accident. Jo was without work. Charles Borelli, a friend of her father, allowed

89 No business in Farnham, in living memory, caused more furore than did the Kentucky Fried Chicken branch in The Borough, which looked up the hill towards Farnham Castle. The face of Col. Sanders was unwelcome here, except by the young and late-night drinkers. Thousands breathed sighs of relief when it was replaced by a branch of Benetton.

90 Only inches beneath the surface, archaeologists are checking an area to the rear of The Borough. The semi-circular stonework, left, was part of the base of the Victorian machinery which turned whalebones to be used in ladies' corsets. The building in which the corsets were made is now the Conservative Club, in Ivy Lane.

91 The Simmonds family at Normandie, Firgrove Hill, in the early 1920s. The elderly gentleman is former Police Superintendent Simmonds. The small boy on his grandmother's knee became Farnham Police's mascot after his father was killed during the final minutes of the First World War. The photographer was Jo Simmonds, whose fiancé was killed three weeks before their wedding.

her to rent the house at the end of Old Kiln Yard, and here she spent hours developing photographs, her hands immersed in the icy cold water she had to use in winter. She remained a very active and articulate spinster until she died aged 88 years.

Both *Seven's Wine Bar* (at 7 The Borough) and the *Queen's Head* (the Farnham pub with the longest history under one livery, Gale's of Horndean) have their own public courtyards to the rear, making a total of 22 courtyards still in use in just two short streets, with almost all of them offering public access.

Until about 200 years ago tolls were

charged at both ends of The Borough, at its junction with Bear (nothing to do with animals, but a corruption of bar) Lane to the east, and at the top of Downing Street, where the *Star* inn, otherwise known as the 'Round House', once stood in the middle of the western end of the thoroughfare. In addition to the yards which existed in the 'controlled by toll' part of the town, there were many in the other main streets as well. Some of the yards behind the Downing Street properties, for example, have been opened up to give customers access to their premises from the rear as well as the front. Alongside R.H. Foster, the cobbler, is a courtyard with a grape-vine growing along one wall, and a hop kiln dated 1854. Downing Street extends round the corner into what seems like part of Union Road, and a charity shop here has facilities for the public to go into its court-yard. Until the River Wey was widened in the 1960s this frequently flooded and the water covered the roads and pavements, often past the greengrocer's and cobbler's shops. You can still see the brackets, at the cobbler's entrance, where boards and sandbags were put, in order to keep some of the flood water out of the building.

At 63 and 64 Downing Street, a modern building has replaced an inn which had been on the site for almost two-and-a-half centuries. Part of the stabling area of the hostelry, which changed its name over the years from the *Adam and Eve* (during which time the tenant, Jonas Jennings, received part of the King's Bounty in 1755 for lodging troops here) to the *King of Prussia*, still remains. Later it became the *Pocket of Hops*, then the *Hop Bag*, and finally the *Downing Street Club* before it closed following a murder outside the building in 1987. This despite the fact that the building faced Farnham's third police station (the first two having been in Bear Lane and Union Road).

92   Three buses and a London coach in Castle Street, one Sunday morning in July 1950. The chimneys can still be seen on Fox's Tower. Wells' Bookshop, left (formerly Kelly's draper's), was owned by the family of John Wells, who was killed in a motorcycle accident three weeks before he was to marry Jo, one of the daughters of Police Supt. Simmonds.

93 Before the River Wey was widened, in the 1960s, sights like this, in Bridge Square, were commonplace around the town. Such flooding was also known to the Saxons, who gave both Gostrey Meadow and an area in East Street known as Dogflud their names. The pub, under the Courage livery, and later to become the *William Cobbett*, was still known as the *Jolly Farmer* at this time.

This courtyard is reputed to be haunted and the screams of a girl, coupled with the sounds of carriage wheels on cobbles, are often said to be heard. The reason seems to be that a young girl was waiting for her betrothed to reach Farnham by carriage from Guildford and heard the wheels rumbling over Longbridge. As the carriage entered the hostelry courtyard the coachman stepped down and told her that it had been held up on the journey and that her loved one had been killed and robbed. The coachman had, however, brought the body to her. It is her screams which are said still to haunt the spot.

Before the present police station, with its murals depicting the town's history, was built in the early 1960s, its site had a long history as a builder's yard. A number of well-known Farnham builders operated from this place, including Birch, Tomsett and Kingham, Mardon and Mills, and Mills and Son. Westwards from this point is the town's largest yard, Wagon Yard. Today it is a car park, but in 1722 Daniel Defoe wrote that he had been told 1,100 wagons a day, each loaded with wheat, had been seen to go into this yard. Farnham was a major wheat centre at that time.

This is the better known of Farnham's two Wagon Yards, and has been the cause of confusion to historians for many years. Until 1998 it was believed that William Willett (1856-1915), the man who had the idea of Daylight Saving, was born in a cottage here.

However, a careful check of the St Andrew's Church baptismal records shows that it was the Wagon Yard off West Street where he first drew breath. He was the son of William and Maria (neé Mason) Willett and was born at Wagon Yard, Beaver's Gardens, West Street. He was baptised on 14 September 1856 at St Andrew's Church. Beavers' Gardens were adjacent to Beaver House, almost opposite what is now the Museum of Farnham.

Until the mid-1960s the present police station site was an area of kilns and outbuildings, occupied by Mardon and Ball, a firm of local builders, and was used as a workshop and store

94 This artistic photograph was taken by Wendy Hobart in Gostrey Meadow during the winter of 1945. The willow trees are bare of leaves, ice can be glimpsed against the river's banks, and the buildings in the background are part of Mills' builders' yard (later demolished for the town's third police station to be built on the site).

95 George Sturt, schoolteacher and author of many books such as *The Wheelwright's Shop* and *Change in the Village*, which have become classics, would have been familiar with this view. It shows the road from the Ridgway down to the Bourne, and was taken about 1890. George Sturt used the name of this village, where he lived, as a pseudonym.

area. In *The Wheelwright's Shop*, George Sturt records that wagons which were staying in town overnight were often kept at this yard, and repaired when necessary. Many of the buildings surrounding the present car park are very old; for example, at 30 and 31 Lower Church Lane constant occupation can be traced for over five hundred years. The New Ashgate Gallery occupies part of the former *Feathers* public house; the iron bracket for the pub sign still sticks out into Lower Church Lane.

Though mostly small, almost every

building on the west side of Downing Street has its yard to the rear. Number 16 was, for many years, a butcher's known as Tarr's. Before that it was Stevenson's gramophone record shop. Despite the advent of modern refrigerated lorries the last owner of Tarr's, a young butcher named Stephen Jones, still used an old trade bicycle for local deliveries and the cycle was kept in the courtyard behind the shop. On the pavement in front of this building is an iron and glass grating. On the metalwork there are a number of horses in relief and the words

'St Pancras'. In the early 1970s an unusual brick was found in a garden in High Park Road, which backs on to Farnham Park. It bore the legend 'St Pancras Iron Works Patent Stable Paviour'. Was there some connection between the owner of the house and the shop, or did the St Pancras Iron Works have a particularly good salesperson in this area?

Almost facing Ivy Lane, which leads to the Conservative Club, is another pair of large wooden gates leading to a courtyard which extends behind several shops. High up on one wall in the yard is probably the oldest piece of painted graffiti in town. Reading 'We want Stevens fish always good', it is believed to have been written by a member of the family of the famous 'Fishy' Stevens, who had a wet and fried fish shop there. In West Street, just round the corner, was a large branch of Macfisheries. Macfisheries staff looking out of their rear windows would have been able to see the written support for 'Fishy' Stevens. Did the originator of the graffiti hope, by it, to annoy the staff of the fish store chain?

West Street abounds with yards, all inhabited. Weaver's Yard is a reminder of the town's wool industry and the making of kersey (a rough cloth), although no evidence for a factory has been found here. However, it is known that sheep grazed in the parish church-yard, just over the wall at the end of Weaver's Yard, so perhaps it was just the sheep which were kept in this yard and the anticipation of weaving their wool gave rise to its name.

Today one of the area's most esteemed architects, Brian Haworth of the Haworth King Partnership, has a practice in Weaver's Yard and Sir Ray Tindle, proprietor of countless newspapers and several radio stations, has his offices above part of it in the large area formerly occupied by Darracott's restaurant and later by the editorial staff of the *Farnham Herald*. Mr. Haworth was an apprentice of the renowned architect Harold Falkner, and remembers his master vividly, particularly the occasion when, owing to leg injuries received

96 Downing Street about a century ago with A.J. Mallam, tailor and breeches maker on the right, where the children are standing. More than 700 years ago this was the route which the monks from Waverley Abbey took on their way to and from Farnham Castle, when they visited the Bishop of Winchester prior to the reformation.

97 Probably the oldest piece of painted graffiti left in Farnham is still visible from the courtyard behind 26 Downing Street. It was intended to annoy the staff at Macfisheries, in West Street, who could see it from their windows. 'Fishy' Stevens operated from the premises in Downing Street on which the words 'We want Stevens fish always good' are painted.

98 Nelson & Goodrick, West Street, *c.*1928. After the London and County Banking Company moved to 38 The Borough, from the left-hand building, Nelson & Goodrick moved in, with Canute and Company, clothiers, next door. N. & G. soon took over Canute's and continued to own both buildings until 40 years ago. Today it is part of Elphicks, with these first-floor windows remaining.

in the First World War, Harold was unable to change gear in his car so drove it to Crondall, three miles away, and back to Farnham, all in second gear!

A number of offices and extensions to their own store have been made in the court-yard behind Elphicks, part of which was once the *Antelope* inn and, as such, needed stabling to its rear. Just past this shop is the footpath which leads to the second largest yard in town, the churchyard.

Farnham is fortunate to have gravestones still encircling the church, the largest parish church in Surrey. In 1856 the cemetery in West Street was opened and burials no longer take place in the churchyard although there is a garden of remembrance in the south-east corner. The most famous grave is that of William Cobbett. It was common in past

centuries for local butchers to graze sheep in this churchyard, but after one tried to keep pigs there and they did 'grave damage' the experiment seems not to have been repeated.

In 1240 a Royal Officer, with his men, had violated the right of sanctuary granted by Waverley Abbey. They dragged a criminal suspect out of the abbey to put him on trial, but this was a serious violation of the abbey's privileges and the officer was publicly scourged in the churchyard, by the Dean and Vicar of Farnham, as a punishment.

In September 1335, the Archdeacon of Surrey, who was also Rector of Farnham, was in dispute with the Bishop of Winchester over financial matters and assaulted the Bishop both physically and verbally in the churchyard after a service. The historian of today can be grateful to Father Etienne Robo for his

99 William Cobbett's tomb, in St Andrew's Churchyard, looking towards the church cottages which once housed the head teachers from St Andrew's School, next door. From *The Corn-Law-Rhymer* comes this verse about Cobbett: 'And in some little lone churchyard, Beside the growing corn, Lay gentle nature's stern prose bard, Her mightiest—peasant born.'

100 An unusual view of the lawn in front of The Rectory, looking towards the parish church. Part of this scene could be viewed from the rear of Weaver's Yard.

scholarly works, including *Medieval Farnham*, where such interesting and often humorous incidents, as well as more scholarly material about Farnham 500 years ago, may be found.

A modern group of offices has been constructed from the William Kingham building, the former wholesale grocer's bacon-smoking and cheese department, and, as if Farnham did not have enough yards, this new unit, first occupied about 1990 and with one wall facing the passage leading to the church-yard, is named simply The Courtyard.

For decades Penfold's Yard, the court-yard in West Street behind architect Harold Falkner's home, gave rear access to the School of Art and housed its caretaker in a cottage there. The stables, which had once been owned by the Penfold family, later became a centre for students of pottery. When the young people moved into their purpose-built art college in The Hart, it was used by mature students who became known as the Farnham Potters.

The Penfold family is also connected with another courtyard in West Street as well as with a crop familiar to many Farnham people—hops. A tea party is recorded in Boswell's *Journals* at which Peckham Williams of Badshot Lea was a guest. He is the man who it is said introduced the Whitebine hop to Farnham. Williams' daughter, Elizabeth, married Miles Poole Penfold in 1786. They owned much property in town, including Cedar Court in Castle Street, and both lived very long lives, Miles dying in 1837 aged 91, and Elizabeth, who inherited his property from him, passing away five years later, aged 96. At that time she was one of the largest landowners in Farnham, holding over three hundred acres. Williams' Yard, almost facing the top of Downing Street, was to the rear of Williams' wine merchants, which is said to have been a family business since 1780. Records show that Anthony Williams, who died in 1802, gave Elizabeth Penfold and John Williams (presumably her brother), of Badshot Place, £50 with which to buy a ring.

At the side entrance of the School of Art, formerly a grammar school for the boys of the town then, early in the 20th century, a school for the girls of wealthy parents, is a blacked-out street lamp, carrying the words 'Evening Classes', above its spiked-top gate. When the girls were here they were instructed always to speak in low tones in the area behind the school, in order not to disturb residents in nearby houses. Games such as tennis were also played here and, according to Win Murphy neé Farr (who, from a school window in this building, saw the flag hoisted on the post office opposite to mark the First World War Armistice), great was the daring required to go through the wicket gate into the caretaker's garden beyond if a ball were accidentally hit there!

The gardens and courtyards of both the *Bishop's Table Hotel* (known for many years as 'Newnham's') and Vernon House (now part of Farnham Library), are well-known and enjoyed by many. What has not been made so public is the fact that there was, about thirty-five years ago, a casino in the grounds of Newnham's, one of several such places in the Farnham area.

The lane at the left of the Museum of Farnham was known for many years as Brewhouse Yard. What is believed to be Farnham's first brewery, with ancillary buildings and cottages for the workers, existed at the end of a long lane and close to a good supply of water from a stream which flowed past many of the gardens on the south side of West Street.

Three of the children of James and Mary Ann Trusler, Charles, Fanny Olivia and William Thomas, were born in a cottage here between 1854 and 1863. Another son, James, was born at Wrecclesham and the youngest, Samuel, was born after the family moved to Loushall Cottage, Dippenhall. In 1873 James and Mary Ann left this country to make a new life in New Zealand. They landed at Dunedin on 10 October 1873, and 125 years to the day after the family landed their descendants held a huge family reunion there in 1998.

101 A scene in a Farnham hop garden before 1873, as that was the date this branch of the Trusler family emigrated to New Zealand. Taken by Froom Photographer, East Street, this photograph was discovered recently, when descendants of James and Mary Anne Trusler held a 125th anniversary reunion, in Dunedin, of the arrival there of their ancestors, on 10 October 1873.

102 Willmer House, left, and Sandford House, fine Georgian houses in West Street. Sandwiched between them is a former brewery. Willmer House, built in 1718, has been used as the town's museum since 1960. Tudor foundations were discovered in its garden in the 1980s. Bishop's Mead, left, formerly Brewhouse Yard, was where James and Mary Anne Trusler lived. They emigrated to New Zealand in 1873.

The land across the road, now occupied by bungalows for senior citizens, was the site of a military college in 1814 which moved to Sandhurst about seven years later. The Farnham building was later demolished and the land sold to William Pink in 1835. In 1839 it was known as College Yard and then as Beaver's Yard before it became College Gardens. Beaver House, built in 1870 and once housing a school, stands on the corner at 79 West Street.

Almost facing Brewhouse Yard (now known as Bishops Mead), is Fox Yard, named after the hostelry which once stood at the corner. Before it became Fox Yard it was Hunter's Yard, named after Thomas Hunter who owned property at this point in 1839.

At the eastern end of this block of buildings is Fenn's Yard, so-called because of the soft drinks (mainly ginger beer) firm which operated from the present Farnham Carpet Company building, part of which backs on to cottages in Fox Yard.

Now renamed Arundell Place and completely redeveloped in the early 1980s, Factory Yard in the 19th century was an area where people who worked in the adjacent sack factory (now 104a West Street) lived. Sail cloth, wagon and rick cloths and hop pockets were all made by those working for John Lidbitter, who transferred his business to this spot from its former factory in what is now St Georges Yard, off Castle Street. By the end of the 19th century there was also a hop kiln and store, both of which faced into Malthouse Yard, where a tallyman's window can still be seen, as well as the large stone and small ironstone setts showing the track taken by carts to and from the hop gardens, which reached down as far as the top of Factory and Malthouse Yards. The cottages in Factory Yard dated from around 1811 and were very basic units. Factory Yard frequently featured in the reports of the Council's Inspector of Nuisances (a euphemism for stench) because of the inadequate, over-

103 This is the only known picture showing, on the far right, the position of *The Fox*, West Street. The pub sign which can be seen on the left is for the *Holly Bush*. Just behind the cart-driver's head is the *Rainbow*, and two buildings farther on is the *Plough*. There was no lack of beer in this 100-yard stretch of West Street!

104 The Salvation Army once had a flourishing group in Farnham. Its members met in a building off West Street, between the present library and museum. Here the Salvation Army Home League is pictured in 1950 and includes two of its stalwarts, Mrs. Medlicott from Heath End, in the floral dress, and Mrs. Gwen Graham, from Lower Church Lane, extreme left.

flowing privies, overcrowding, and diseases such as diphtheria and enteric fever.

The remains of iron hinges on which gates were hung can be seen on a wall inside an archway between 110 and 111 West Street, indicating the entrance to another courtyard. The building's original structure, later re-fronted, can easily be seen under the arch. Then comes Lion and Lamb Yard which, despite its appearance is, for the most part, one of the town's most recently constructed courtyards.

Even the cut brick plaque, dated 1537 (possibly the date of the original buildings), is set into a wall which was only constructed by John Kingham in the early 1920s.

During the 16th, 17th and 18th centuries there was an inn on this site known for a long time as the *White Hart* but changing to the *Lion and Lamb* sometime between 1692 and 1720. In the early 19th century this was one of Farnham's principal coaching inns, where the *Tally Ho*, the *Independent* and the *New Times* stopped at 2.30 p.m. every day, except for Sundays, *en route* to Portsmouth from London. Thomas Mathews, who was the landlord at the *Lion and Lamb* in the mid-19th century, also had a brewery at the site. In 1855 Thomas Mathews and his father, also Thomas, bought the *Duke of Cambridge* public house in East Street.

The Farnham Printing Company had their machines in a building in this yard for many years, and in the 1930s a business known as The Weavers also operated from here. Visitors to the area who dined in the Lion and Lamb tearooms opposite took the woven items back to London and to many parts of the world.

The barn now occupied by Laura Ashley was once a garage for cars and vans belonging to the wholesale grocer, William Kingham and Son. Some of the staff of this firm lived in wooden cottages built on low stilts, which faced the barn. More than half the retail and office units in this yard were completed in 1986 and were officially opened by Virginia Bottomley M.P., wearing Victorian clothing, in November of that year. The carved figures of the lion and the lamb, much-loved by children who clamber over them when visiting the courtyard, are the work of sculptor Edwin Russell, and the piece was commissioned by the Ellis Campbell Group especially for the shopping courtyard development.

Hart's Yard, to the side of the *Farnham Herald* office, leads to the forge where, in the early years of the 20th century, iron stoves were made to be retailed in F. Hart's ironmonger's shop at 117 West Street. The large stones set against the wall at ground level, and going up the yard, were to protect the walls from the cartwheels. In 1924 the printing works of the *Farnham Herald* was extended and lettering above a door shows this date. Past the forge, and leading into one of the three 'prongs' of Long Garden Walk, is another very old building, Daniel Hall, which has been used for many years as a centre for the Scout movement in Farnham. Robert Baden-Powell, the movement's founder, was frequently seen in Farnham in the 1930s, when he lived at Pax Hill, Bentley. Backing on to Daniel Hall, and to the rear of the present Argos store, is the premises which once had a swinging sign representing an iron fish, the publishing office of *Fishing News*.

Ten

For King and Country

THERE ARE TWO FEATURES of the First World War which are directly connected with Farnham: the first is the Christian organisation known as Toc H, and the second is the Two-Minute Silence.

Bishop Talbot and his wife saw two sons leave for the Western Front but only one return. Lieut. Gilbert Walter Lyttleton Talbot, the younger of the two, was in charge of a platoon of the 7th Rifle Brigade at Flanders which was virtually wiped out. Gilbert died on 31 July 1915.

His brother, Neville, later founded a soldiers' institute at Poperinghe and named it Talbot House after his late brother. It was a home-from-home for men who were fighting and needed a few hours respite. The only rule was that all rank should be abandoned once inside the building. The men could read, write home, have food and baths and, in the attic, attend church services. Soon the signallers abbreviated Talbot House to Toc H (it was much shorter to send in morse code); its symbol was a small, burning oil lamp. Although the Rev. Tubby Clayton is the name indelibly associated in people's minds with Toc H, the organisation would not have existed without the death of a Farnham man.

When the war began, on Tuesday 4 August 1914, the railway between Bordon and Aldershot (military towns between which Farnham was sandwiched) was immediately commandeered by the War Office and around fifty men from the 4th City of London Territorial Regiment were moved in to guard the length of track. Sentries were posted on the platforms and along the line and many people thought the area had been infiltrated by Germans. On 6 August a suspected German spy was arrested at Farnham station. A tall fair-haired man had been seen on the platform taking photographs and writing in a notebook. He was locked in the waiting room and then marched down South Street and into The Borough, where the photographs in his camera were examined at Hales the Photographers. When his notebook was examined he was found to be a practical joker from Guildford who had been writing a letter whilst waiting for a train; when he realised he was being eyed suspiciously he wrote in the letter, 'I suppose they are taking me for a German spy.' He was later released but not before the story had spread around the town like wildfire, embellished with each re-telling.

The *Farnham Herald* published lists of names, every week, of the men from the town who had enlisted in the army. They included H.C. Patrick, who owned the town's largest undertaker's business and was later to supply hundreds of headstones for British soldiers' graves in France and Belgium, Frank Swain, one of the owners of Swain and Jones' garage in East Street, founded seven years earlier, E.F. Crundwell, solicitor, Tommy Simmonds, son of the police superintendent, and G.R.R. Combe, only son of Mr. Richard and The Lady Constance Combe, from Pierrepont, Frensham. Within four weeks, 328 men from Farnham aged between 18 and 30 had regis-

105 J.H. Dodman, Post Office, Frensham, published this First World War postcard of one of the village boys, home on leave. The young soldier is believed to be a member of the Nash family, who lived and worked for Mr. Richard and The Lady Constance Combe on the Pierrepont Estate.

tered for military service at the recruiting office in the Corn Exchange, Castle Street.

By September the *Farnham Herald* had started to list the casualties, and large houses such as The Hill at Gong Hill and several in Shortheath and Rowledge were turned into army hospitals. Waverley Abbey House was accepted by the War Office as an annexe to the Cambridge Military Hospital in Aldershot, and by 24 September the first 17 wounded officers were moved into the house adjacent to Waverley Abbey. In October 1916 the *Daily*

Mirror featured this hospital in its pages complete with photographs of Mrs. Rupert Anderson, who owned the property, and her four daughters, all of whom were nurses. Two years later Mrs. Anderson was awarded an O.B.E. for services at the Waverley Hospital.

At the same time as the wounded officers were being taken to Waverley Abbey House, the first of a large group of men who had volunteered for Kitchener's Army arrived at Farnham station before marching to Frensham Common, where they lived in tents and trained, prior to being sent overseas. In the town, 3,000 men of the King's Liverpool Regiment (an overspill from Aldershot) were billeted in private homes and empty houses. Soldiers' canteens were opened in the Corn Exchange and in church halls. Food was in short supply and when the civic restaurant opened on 26 February 1918, in Church House, it was an immediate success. Soon an average of £24 per week was being taken from around 250 daily customers, from all walks of life.

The local bus service was operated by Aldershot and District Traction Company from its depot in Halimote Road, Aldershot. The bus drivers did not always stick to the speed limit of 12 m.p.h. in outlying areas and 10 m.p.h. in town, and in 1918 they were told the journey between Farnham and Aldershot should not take less than 30 minutes. Today, with vastly more traffic congestion, the time-table allows 15 minutes for this journey.

It was debated whether or not German prisoners-of-war should be given the task of cleaning out the river bed of the Wey, and a Canadian Forestry Unit felled many trees at Crooksbury Hill for war purposes. This is described by George Sturt in *The Wheelwright's Shop*:

> The trees, cut into lengths, stripped of their bark and stacked in piles, gave to many an erstwhile secluded hillside a staring publicity. This or that quiet place, the home of peace, was turned into a ghastly battlefield, with the naked and maimed corpses of trees lying about.

It was the same George Sturt that Mr. J. Alfred Eggar, an estate agent, told of his idea for a Two-Minute Silence, now an Armistice Day ritual, originating in his Castle Street office during the preliminaries for the Farnham Fair on 10 May 1916. Bishop Talbot and Archbishop Davidson had both refused to support the idea but Canon Cunningham helped Mr. Eggar make the event a success. Eventually it was adopted by the government and a letter of thanks from the Home Secretary was sent to J.A.E.

Winifred Farr, a 12-year-old at Farnham Girls' Grammar School, then in West Street, was the first person in that educational establishment to know the Armistice agreement had been signed. Her desk was next to the window and she saw the Union Jack being hoisted on the flagpole of the post office (an agreed sign for peace), which was almost opposite.

In October 1916, Joseph King M.P. had voiced his opinion that, after the present war, Germany would quickly recover and, at some

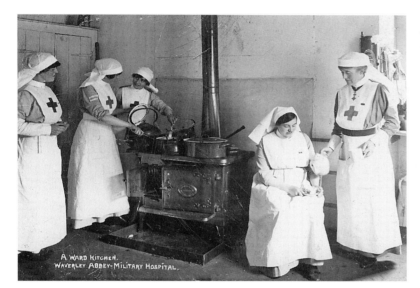

A WARD KITCHEN. WAVERLEY ABBEY-MILITARY HOSPITAL.

106 During the First World War Waverley Abbey House was one of many large houses around Farnham taken over as military hospitals. This postcard shows a ward kitchen and what looks like a Kitchener stove, on which are heavy iron utensils. A fire extinguisher is behind the oldest nurse's head, but other equipment is minimal.

107 An Armistice Day parade in the late 1960s, and members of the Farnham Red Cross march down Downing Street to the parish church. Baxter's, Lipton's and the International Stores have long since left the scene, although Curry's remains. Note the three bays and gate of International's shop-front; it is now one long glass window.

future date, inflict another bloodbath on humanity. The editor of the *Farnham Herald* wrote that this must be prevented, whether it was in 60, 100 or even 200 years time. In the event it was only 20 years after all the ends of the First World War had been tied up that the Second World War began, with Germany as the instigator.

On 2 September 1939 the National Service Act was passed and all British men aged 20-22 years were called up for duty. War with Germany was announced the following day and a few weeks later ration books were distributed. The censor was busy making certain that no information was printed or broadcast which might help the enemy, so local newspapers reported veiled information such as, 'A very noisy bomb, known as the landmine type, fell in the vicinity of a children's convalescent home in the southern counties,' even though everybody locally knew it was an incident which had taken place in Farnham.

The *Farnham Herald* for 9 September 1939 reports that a number of hop pickers had failed to turn up for work at Tice's hop gardens, in Badshot Lea. It was thought their non-appearance may have been due to the fear of possible air raids and a lack of shelter in the open fields.

108 Private Harry Farr, shot for cowardice, was one of 307 shell-shocked soldiers executed by British firing squads during the First World War. Perhaps one of Farnham's citizens, his granddaughter Janet Booth, who has campaigned for many years, will eventually succeed in gaining a pardon for these traumatised young men.

109 Arnold and Comben, Abbott's, Heath and Wiltshire, Swain and Jones—the list of Farnham's motor firms in the early years of the 20th century is considerable. Warren & Co. Ltd., from Wrecclesham, although very good in its time, is an 'also-ran' in the list of the famous. This advertisement is taken from *The Homeland Handbook*, published in 1914.

110 The Bishop of Winchester unveiled the war shrine in The Bourne on 19 May 1917.

Farnham Girls' Grammar School's autumn term was postponed when it was found, on 1 September, that no air-raid shelters had been constructed at the new school building in Menin Way, which had been formally opened only six weeks earlier. The Surrey Education Committee was, naturally, reluctant to allow children to go to a school where there was no protection from air attacks, but the headmistress, Miss Frances Wake King, persuaded those in authority that the school's boiler room, which was partly underground, would be a safe enough place to shelter up to 40 girls and staff. Term began on 19 September with part-time schooling in the building and home study for the rest of the day until the air-raid shelters were completed a month later. From being a school to which it was deemed unsafe to go at the beginning of the academic year, before the end of it, the local girls were joined by those from the Greycoat Hospital School, Westminster, with their head-mistress, Miss Chetham-Strode. By this time Farnham had been declared by the authorities a safe or reception area. The buildings were so spacious it was possible for both the Greycoat and F.G.G.S. pupils to attend lessons every day, each school alternating mornings and afternoons while the pupils of one school occupied the classrooms and hall in the normal way, the other held classes in Shide House, a property specially purchased in Menin Way, in cloakrooms, the cleaner's cupboard, or anywhere else space could be found. (Menin Way itself is connected with the First World War—the son of the builder of the houses having been killed in that war and his name inscribed on the Menin Gate.)

In January 1940 call-up was extended to men aged up to 27 years and by May this was extended to those up to 36 years of age. The old soldiers, those who had served in the First World War, felt strongly that they should do their bit, and many joined the Local Defence Volunteers (L.D.V.), known locally as 'Look, Duck and Vanish'. On 9 July the L.D.V. became the Home Guard. In its issue for 8 June 1940 the *Farnham Herald* published the L.D.V.s weekly programme of activities: Monday 8-9 p.m. general talk and guard duties, Tuesday 7-9 p.m. miniature range (shooting practice), Wednesday 8-9 p.m. musketry, Friday guard, general duties and musketry. Guard was mounted every day at 9.30 p.m. Most of the L.D.V. members were older businessmen and teachers, who must have found it tiring to work all day, be on duty all night then work the next day.

111 Home Guard and Special Constabulary at William Kingham & Sons, in September 1941. Centre, with strap across his chest, is Kenneth Kingham, one of the firm's partners. Surnames of others include: Lovelock, Bentick, Poulter, Bramley, Hawkins, Gregory, Eade, Corrigan, Barrett, Scarff, Coles, Parker, Towns, Osborne, Mutch, Harding, Painter, Fry, Hart, Spence, Taylor, Stout, Silver, Stitchman, Richardson, Johnson, Rogers, Green, Smart, Hole and Kemp.

In his privately published family history, *Entanglements*, R.E. Hack devotes a chapter to the Farnham Home Guard (and its predecessor the L.D.V.) and other voluntary units, including the A.R.P., W.R.V.S., Red Cross, St John Ambulance and Salvation Army. An upstairs room of Abbotts Motor Works at Wrecclesham was one of the meeting places for such organisations. Mr. Hack recalls:

> The Wrecclesham Unit first assembled, one cannot say paraded, in the office upstairs at Abbotts ... Our total weaponry being one sword, shotgun (no cartridges) and a Match (SMLE) Service Rifle .303 with one 5-round clip of dummy ammunition, and just to terrify the enemy we were issued with canvas arm-bands lettered L.D.V.

Later in the war the Farnham Home Guard were provided with a Northover Projector, a strange device which would fire a bottle filled with phosphorus. The idea was that it should set a tank on fire. Mr. Hack continues:

> Initially intended to have no organisation or rank, these things happened and were made official and incorporated using the former Territorial Army set-up and the County Regiment status. Farnham was constituted A Company, located in the Drill Hall in Bear Lane with a Headquarters Platoon based on the postal workers, and six others, of which Wrecclesham became No.1 Platoon.

The Commanding Officer of Farnham's A Company was Major Patrick, not only the principal partner of the town's largest undertaker,

112 Air-raid wardens, Service Sector 10/11, in the back garden of Sandford House, West Street, in 1940. The building was the home of the Rev. Bird (wearing a white helmet). Others in the photograph include: Mr. Whitington, C. Dimes, W. Gibson, Mr. Green jnr., A. Green, Arthur Dean, P. Beagley, W. Wilkinson, F. Brockhurst, Mr. Beeson, Mr. Alwyn and Miss Groft.

113 Some of Farnham's Second World War Civil Defence personnel, from the St Cross area. Back row, left to right, are: R. Fry, W. Martin, W. Macklin, Charlie Dean, Jack Watts, A. Harris, A. Jarman, J. Crumpett. Front row: C. Constant, Doreen Baker, Eileen Watts (later married Dennis Stone), Jim Kimber, Mrs. Marples, Mrs. Bishop, Charlie Holdship.

but also a crack shot who, prior to the outbreak of war, competed in the King's Prize at Bisley. His adjutant was Captain Townsend, who had been a major in the First World War, and the transport officer was Lt. (formerly Rear Admiral) Mather. The man in charge of food for this motley company was a Boer War veteran, Mr. Harmes, the baker from Sandrock Hill. Platoon No. 6 was made up of workers at Crosby's West Street factory, under the direction of Lieut. Basil Crosby. The dummy bomb on which his team learned bomb disposal techniques was unearthed during building work on the site in 1998, and the town was sealed off while the device was investigated by the army bomb disposal unit who found it was as safe then as it had been almost sixty years earlier.

One mysterious incident involving the Home Guard concerned an officer, one of the town's bank managers, who was killed by a mortar in the Bear Lane Drill Hall. An official enquiry was held, but no reason could be found for the death, so a Lloyds Bank manager had a funeral with full military honours.

Female workers at the Crosby factory were issued with green bib-and-brace dungarees and a triangular piece of yellow cloth to tie round their heads. At an exhibition to commemorate the 50th anniversary of the war's end, one of Crosby's former workers wrote:

> It was very noisy with continuous banging and hammering and the atmosphere was full of sawdust. We made boxes for all the different sized shells—green for the army, blue for the navy. They were made of the best quality wood—teak, oak and mahogany. Some girls wrote notes and put them in the boxes. We didn't get any replies—I think they took the notes out when they put the shells in.
>
> The girls working on boxes were given a pint of milk a day as it was believed it would help with the fumes. We worked from 7.30 a.m. to 6 p.m. Monday to Friday and half-a-day on Saturday—even Christmas Day. We were allowed two tea breaks of 10 minutes each. We were allowed to take home scrap wood for the fire. Mother was grateful for that. We listened to 'Music While You Work' over the Tannoy. In 1944 we watched the army lorries. The convoys went past without break for days and nights before the invasion of Normandy. The lorries were hidden under the trees and camouflaged, around Runfold, Crooksbury and in the countryside. Towards the end of the war production switched to making doors and fittings for prefab houses.

During both First and Second World Wars many Canadian soldiers were billeted in the Farnham area, and one nissen hut in which they trained, in Bishop's Mead, is still in use today as a garage. Officers carried out their duties in Willmer House, later to become Farnham's museum, and others stayed in large houses throughout the area. Captain Robert L. Carter, an officer billeted at The Warren, Heath End, wrote a poem called 'Memories' in the autograph book of Peggy Read, a young girl from Hale. After writing about Hale at Christmas, New Year, August Bank Holiday and V.J. Day, Robert Carter included the lines: 'No! These are not the only memories, To be taken back, far across the sea—However short

the rations, here was Home, A fireside, easy chair, a cup of tea.' Peggy, who later married John Chapman, remains in contact with Robert Carter, and the last holiday she had with her late husband was to Canada to visit her wartime friend.

In the middle of June 1941, the *Farnham Herald* carried a story about Lt.-Cmdr. Geoffrey Carver R.N., H.M.S. *Dorsetshire*, who was said to have fired the three torpedoes which sank the *Bismarck*, pride of the German navy. He was the second son of Mr. and Mrs. S. Carver of Highlands, Shortheath. Lt.-Cmdr. Carver is quoted as saying, When my orders came to stand by to sink her with torpedoes, the *Bismarck* appeared to be on fire from stem to stern.

From 1939 to 1944 the residents of Farnham invested over £3 million of small savings in regular commitments. Despite this they were determined to raise an extra £210,000 during 'Salute the Soldier Week' in June 1944. The money was to be used to equip and maintain a brigade of airborne troops. The target was reached and so Farnham people acknowledged the army as well as the navy and air force, for whom record sums had already been raised in 'Warships' and 'Wings for Victory' weeks. Two of the fund-raising events for 'Salute the Soldier' in Farnham were a production of *The Charcoal Burner's Son*, held at Wrecclesham Village Hall, and a programme of sports events for young people and service personnel arranged by Brigadier L.A. Fanshaw and Mr. F.G. James.

Much of Farnham Park was dug up in order that crops could be grown there, a base was built at the park's Bear Lane entrance to carry a large gun directed up South Street, and in Farnham Castle a camouflage development unit was set up. Many well-known artists worked there making camouflage patterns which it was hoped would confuse the enemy. One of these was John Hutton, also renowned for his glass engraving. Mr. Hutton became friendly with Basil Crosby and often

114 Many villages around Farnham gave certificates to those residents of theirs who had served in the armed forces during the Second World War, and Badshot Lea was no exception.

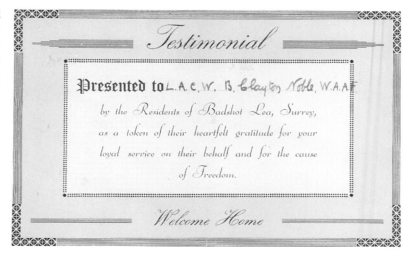

Testimonial

Presented to L.A.C.W. B. Clayton Noble. W.A.A.F.

by the Residents of Badshot Lea, Surrey,

as a token of their heartfelt gratitude for your

loyal service on their behalf and for the cause

of Freedom.

Welcome Home

visited his West Street factory. While there he painted a number of pictures depicting both men and women at work and four of the paintings are now on show in Farnham's public library.

The work produced at Crosby's was held in high esteem by the staff at the War Office and the company continued to be granted contracts for items such as collapsible assault craft and Bailey Bridge pontoons long after the war ended. During the war many workers in the Crosby factory whose homes were too far away to travel back to at night lived in tents in the fields behind the buildings.

Miss Rosie Turner, an employee at the company, was selected by her fellow workers to be 'Miss Ta of Farnham', and on 8 July 1944, in Gostrey Meadow, she said 'thankyou' to seamen at the inaugural ceremony for Seamen's Services Week. Farnham Grammar School adopted H.M.S. *Farnham Castle*, a ship which escorted Russian convoys for the last few months of the war.

On Christmas Eve 1944, Mrs. Violet Horne received a card from her husband, Sergeant Horne, who was a Japanese prisoner-of-war. It had taken almost a year to reach her. Six months later, the day after Victory in Europe was declared, Sergeant Harry

Pickford R.A. arrived back home in Hale, having escaped from the German prisoner-of-war camp in which he had been held for four years.

Maurice Elphick, one of the sons of the owners of the family outfitter and drapery firm of West Street, served in the army, navy and air force in the Second World War. Born in 1918, he was educated at Farnham Grammar School. In 1941 he married Barbara and the couple had three children, Michael, Elizabeth and Allan. Maurice was loved and respected by people in all walks of life, and tributes were paid to him by countless organisations and charities with which he was involved when he died in November 1998. These were succinctly summed up by the *Surrey and Hants News* who reported a former member of his shop's staff, upon hearing of his death, saying of him, 'He was a real gentleman'.

Another Farnham Grammar School pupil (1927-34) who distinguished himself in the Second World War was Alan Smallman. Now known as Brigadier Alan Smallman M.B.E., he was Brigade Major in the Commandos in 1942 and was later at the Staff College, Camberley, the War Office and Eastern Command. He served as the Town Mayor of Farnham from 1984-6.

115 The late Maurice Elphick took a keen interest in local history and business. He was loved and respected by the townsfolk as well as by staff in his family firm. He named some of the Farnham Chamber of Commerce (1928/9) in this photograph taken on Alexandra Rose Day: Humphrey Elphick (his brother), Owen Crundwell, George Hale, Vic Comben and Lionel Smith.

At the exhibition in town marking the 50th anniversary of the end of the war, an anonymous Farnham fireman recalled:

The most famous fire [in Farnham] was at Church House in Union Road. It was a disaster because it was in the middle of the night. [The building] was occupied by the Canadian army. They blamed a record player for starting the fire. I also attended when two bombs dropped in Firgrove Hill. An aircraft had been trying to bomb the railway line but it missed and hit a house. There was damage but no casualties. I helped rescue two people. Farnham firemen were also sent to the London, Southampton and Portsmouth blitzes.

Frensham Ponds gave enemy aircraft a sense of direction, especially in moonlight, so they were drained. Frensham Common was used as a tank training ground before going to France. The Hog's Back was crowded with tanks prior to the invasion [of Normandy] because it's chalk and the tanks didn't get bogged down.

Black Lake Sawmills and the one at Churt were manned by German PoWs. They had a grey uniform with a big red patch. Prisoners were also kept at Lloyd George's estate at Churt.

In common with the rest of the country, there was much rejoicing in Farnham on 8 May 1945. On 9 May, bowls, tennis and swimming in Gostrey Meadow and Brightwell's Gardens were free to all, and in the evening around 500 people joined in dancing and community singing there. On V.E. Day itself, though, peace was celebrated in a more spontaneous way. Mrs. Ruby Clayton, from Roman Way, recalled in 1995:

> We didn't have a party but oh, it was such a wonderful day. My husband, Stan, my dad and brothers were all in the *Duke of Cambridge* (in East Street). We lived in Stoke Hills then. I was with them and as soon as they announced peace everyone went out into the street.

We were singing and dancing—all the old songs—and we were about eight in a line across the road. We went all along East Street singing, then up Castle Street and along High Park Road and back to Stoke Hills. All the way we sang and danced. People were shouting out from every house. 'It's 'peace, it's peace,' they cried. Look, there are tears in my eyes. It makes me like that to remember. Everyone was so happy then.

After the end of the Second World War a number of small factories began to be opened on trading estates just outside the town. They

116 Crondall firemen in brass hats have stopped outside the *Plume of Feathers* to the delight of onlookers, three small boys, one young girl and an elderly man. The *Plume* was under the Courage livery in the 1930s, when this photograph was taken, and much of the beer sold in the pub was brewed in Alton.

117 Bowling has long been a popular pastime, with Farnham having at least three clubs. The reason for this gathering outside the club-house in High Park Road in the 1930s is not known, but it is obviously a ladies' event. All the members are wearing white hats and are supported by a number of others, all sporting summer 'straws'.

118 Some of the old and interesting buildings, at 93-5 East Street, which were demolished in the 1960s to make way for The Woolmead development. Probably photographed by Edward Griffith, H.C. Patrick, the undertaker, moved his business farther eastwards, to the junction with St Cross Road. At that time traffic in this thoroughfare was still two-way.

119 The Bristol and West Building Society (formerly the Farnham Benefit Building Society), at 98 East Street, and the Betta Cleaners and Betta Wool Shop (96 and 97) were all demolished over thirty years ago as part of The Woolmead development scheme.

produced almost everything, from sweets at Dickson Orde, clothes horses at Plastic Coatings, and radio and hi-fi components at Sound Sales, to toiletries at Thomas Christy's (which was originally in Bear Lane).

The construction of Farnham by-pass began in the 1930s and with it the saga of the traffic at Hickley's Corner. Farnham town centre streets are too narrow to accommodate the heavy traffic which thunders through them each day, and with more listed buildings here than historic Chester (according to Waverley Borough Council), the vibration from these vehicles could be having a severely detrimental effect.

After what most people now agree was an inappropriate development in East Street (the Woolmead) in the 1960s, and the demolition of the town's only major Art Deco building, the Regal Cinema, in the late 1980s, more care is being taken over building design and regulations. The St Georges complex between Castle Street and Bear Lane (which replaced a number of buildings including the old Drill Hall and Demuth's Toiletries), the Lion and Lamb Yard extension, and the new offices and homes in Borelli Yard have all enhanced their neighbouring, listed, buildings rather than detracting from them.

Eleven

Tinker, Tailor, Soldier

THERE ARE MANY PEOPLE who live or have lived in Farnham who have a claim to fame. John Michael Hawthorn, better known as Mike Hawthorn was the first person to bring the World Motor Racing Driving Championship to this country, in 1958. Unfortunately he was killed a few months later, on 22 January 1959, just outside Guildford. He is buried in West Street Cemetery and there is a racing car on his tombstone with the words 'A gay and gallant sportsman' beneath the formal inscription. His first home in Farnham was at 4, Osborn Road, but his family later moved to Greenfields, Folly Hill. He was educated at Barfield School, Runfold, the former home of John Henry Knight, another man with motoring connections.

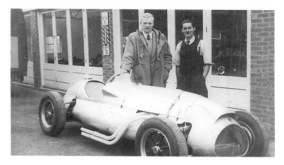

120 In addition to being, at one time, this country's best racing driver, Mike Hawthorn also wrote *Challenge me the Race* and *Champion Year*. Here he stands, left, outside his family's garage in East Street, with Brit Pearce, his mechanic, and an unpainted Cooper Bristol. In 1952 Mike won three races in one day at Goodwood, on his debut with this car.

121 In this photograph Mike Hawthorn can be seen in a Jaguar car, VDU 881, the vehicle which, according to motoring writer and author, Doug Nye, was the one he was driving on the day of his untimely death. Here Mike is racing at Silverstone in 1958.

122 John Henry Knight, with one of his sons, on the petrol-driven car which he invented and had built at 50 West Street. In his *Reminiscences of the Motor Car Movement*, JHK records the incident which led to the first fine for a traffic offence, and also says he believes John Pullinger, his employee, was the earliest chauffeur in England.

123 An interior view of Heath and Wiltshire's garage in West Street, almost opposite the *Jolly Sailor*, taken in 1921. At this time the company hand built car bodies on Ford chassis. Percy Dean, brother of Arthur (third from left), went overnight by train to Manchester, collected a chassis and, sitting on a wooden bench, drove it back to Farnham.

John Henry Knight, inventor, author and photographer, was born at Weybourne House, a magnificent Georgian building a few yards away from a public house which until 1998 had been known for more than a century as the *Elm Tree*. It was named after a huge tree that once stood at the nearby crossroads and which had been photographed on many occasions by JHK. He designed many machines including one of the first petrol-driven motor cars, which was built at his workshop at 50 West Street in 1895. Together with his driver, Mr. Pullinger, he received on 17 October of that year what is believed to be the first fine in this country for a traffic offence. Because Mr. Pullinger was driving what was called a loco-motive, out of permitted hours and without a licence, both he and the vehicle's owner, John Henry Knight, were fined half-a-crown each. The vehicle was only allowed to move at two miles per hour in town and four miles an hour in the country. He was also a brilliant photo-grapher, wrote several books, and constructed a number of engines, including an automatic brick wall building machine, a wooden-sprung tyre and a large sling for throwing missiles. When he died, Knight opted to be buried in the churchyard at St John's, Hale, now only feet away from one of the greatest traffic bottlenecks in the area.

124 The elm tree from which the nearby public house took its name until 1998, when the *Elm Tree* became the *Cob and Pen* (or 'couple of old ducks' as an elderly resident was heard to say after the name change). The tree stands at the Weybourne Lanes/Weybourne Road junction. The washing blows at the entrance to the present Millstream.

125 Britain holds the accolade for the invention of the hovercraft. When it went through Farnham in August 1959, *en route* to the Farn-borough Air Show it caused quite a stir. A bus stop road marking, on the right, shows that two-way traffic was still allowed in this stretch of The Borough.

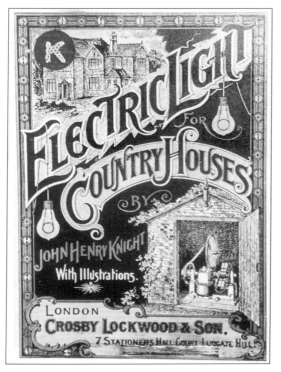

126 *Electric Light for Country Houses* by John Henry Knight, with illustrations, was just one of several books written by the versatile and extremely intelligent man who was also responsible for many inventions, including a petrol-driven car and a 'trench bomb thrower'—a wooden engine similar to a Roman ballista—which lobbed a missile up to 130 yards.

127 The little girl who, as Vera Lynn, became the 'Forces' Sweetheart' in the Second World War, spent every summer of her childhood at Weybourne. She still visits Farnham and wrote about Weybourne, the *Six Bells* and the *Bush Hotel* in her autobiography. Here, in Hammicks, Lion and Lamb Yard, she is signing copies of *We'll Meet Again*.

It was at one of the corner shops near Weybourne House that two well-known women bought sweets and other small items. One was Jessie Matthews, star of stage, screen and radio, her most famous role on the latter being the principal character in *Mrs. Dale's Diary*. Jessie lived at a house called 'Evergreen' (named after a stage show in which she appeared), on the north side of Weybourne Road, a site close to the county border and now occupied by a small housing development which backs on to Rowhills Copse. For a while Jessie Matthews held the licence of *The Alliance*, a town centre public house which is

now an estate agent's office at the top of Downing Street.

The other Weybourne shopper was Dame Vera Lynn, the 'Forces' Sweetheart' in the Second World War. As a child she spent at least a month every year staying with an aunt who lived in one of the group of houses to the east of the Upper/Lower Weybourne Lanes and Weybourne Road junction. She mentions the corner shop, run by Vi Mason, in her autobiography and also recalls that when she was in the sticky and almost unbearable heat of Burma during the war, it was memories of the cool taste of water taken from a well near Weybourne, a mile from Farnham, which sustained her. She also had happy memories of walks across the fields for lemonade outside the *Six Bells*.

Despite being 35 miles away from the sea, Farnham has several nautical connections. The subject of 'Bubbles', the painting used in the Pears' Soap advertisement, later became Admiral Sir William James, who lived at Churt and kept his head of curly hair to the end of his long life. The young William was painted by Sir John Millais, who had many relations living in this area. John Ridgway, a paratrooper who, together with colleague Chay Blyth, rowed the Atlantic in *English Rose III* in 1966, lived in Middle Church Lane. David Johnstone, a journalist with the *Surrey and Hants News*, lost his life undertaking the same challenge.

Despite its proximity to Aldershot, Farnham does not have many connections with the army, although had it not been for the fact that Major Richard Toplady and his pregnant wife were visiting Farnham in 1740 (more than a century before Aldershot was founded as the Home of the British Army), young Augustus, the author of the hymn *Rock of Ages*, might not have been born in this town, in a former building on what is now part of Elphick's premises.

A familiar army officer frequently seen collecting his pension at Farnham Post Office was Field Marshal Montgomery, who bought Isington Mill, just outside Farnham, soon after the Second World War ended. George 'Paddy' Miles, known as 'the Good Samaritan' by the poor people of the town, was an army officer before becoming a general practitioner in Farnham. His nickname was the result of his endearing trait of 'forgetting' to send bills to those he knew were unable to pay without great hardship to themselves and their family. When he died, these people collected farthings and halfpennies and paid to have a seat made in his memory, which incorporated a carving of the parable of the Good Samaritan. Originally this was situated near his surgery, in East Street, but later it was moved to Brightwell's Gardens.

128 Farnham's proximity to Aldershot, home of the British Army for almost 150 years, has resulted in many army officers living in this town. Possibly the most famous was 'Monty', Field Marshal Viscount Montgomery of Alamein, (second left) who lived at Isington Mill but shopped and collected his pension (in a chauffeur-driven car) each week in Farnham.

Sid Towns, who spent his entire life in the town, is one of the very few Farnham old soldiers who has been privileged enough to enter the Chelsea Royal Hospital of Pensioners. Before he left his Middle Church Lane home, for London, his neighbours held a party for him in the parish churchyard, a place facing his home and onto which his windows looked. When he returns to this town, on holiday, wearing his scarlet and black traditional Chelsea Pensioner uniform, he brings a brightness to the streets which is not equalled by the fashions of the 1990s.

129 Sid Towns, Farnham-born and bred, on holiday in his home town, now that he is a pensioner at the Royal Hospital, Chelsea. He is standing in Lower Church Lane, the narrow street with a gutter in the centre. Apart from the road marking, this picture could have been taken any time since the advent of photography over 150 years ago.

A man who was a legend in his own time was the tall, elderly gentleman who came from The Bourne, where his father had been a policeman. In the late 1940s and throughout the following decade, he was frequently seen and even more often heard, as he strode the streets of the town, right arm stretched in front of him and fist clenched, shouting, 'Up the Red Army.' He ended his days in a home for the elderly in Hale Road, but 'Old Bill'— William Warr—is still remembered with affection by many people, almost forty years after his strident tones were last heard.

Old Bill's father would have been subordinate to Superintendent Simmonds at Farnham Police Station, the building facing Gostrey Meadow and adjacent to Church House in Union Road. Supt. Simmonds was much loved and when, following a fall from his horse, he lay in his room at the police station, with leeches, brought specially from London, taking blood from a damaged area of his brain, a public subscription paid for straw to be strewn on the part of the road within earshot of his home so that horse hooves and cartwheels would not disturb him. Two other long-serving police officers were Supt. Roy Goacher and Supt. Trusler, whose daughter, Linda, now owns Lloyd and Keyworth Music in Downing Street.

Those people who tune in their televisions to a test card might see a Farnham girl, Carol Hersee, sitting with a toy clown in the centre of Test Card C. She has been sitting in the same place for over thirty years.

Almost two centuries separate Farnham's two most famous cricketers, 'Silver' Billy Beldham, county and England player, and Graham Thorpe. 'Silver' Billy, wearing a stovepipe hat, can be seen on a pub sign at *The Cricketers* in Wrecclesham, where there is also a street named after him, Beldham Road. Graham Thorpe, who also has cricketing brothers and is a county and England player, comes from Wrecclesham as well.

Possibly the earliest of the 'popular' authors to have either lived at, been born in,

130 Farnham Cricket Club's batsmen began scoring runs in 1782, and there was no batsman better than William 'Silver Billy' Beldham, who was born in Wrecclesham and is pictured here in 1850, aged 84—12 years before his death. The F.C.C.'s first home was constructed by Beldham, in 1791, at Holt Pound and it remains there today, behind the *Forest Inn*.

131 William 'Silver Billy' Beldham's cricket bat, which he used more than 200 years ago, when playing for Farnham Cricket Club. The club played its first game on 13 August 1782 against Odiham Cricket Club. In that match Beldham scored 17 runs, the third highest score of the day.

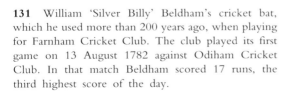

132 Julian Critchley, author, journalist and politician, lived in both Castle Street and Bridge Square, Farnham, although the constituency he represented was Aldershot. When he was at the latter address he was living opposite to where William Cobbett, also an author, journalist and M.P., had been born—a public house which honoured Julian by naming its pet tarantula after him.

William Cobbett (1763-1835) was born at the *Jolly Farmer Inn*. He had no formal education but he had a father who taught him to read and write and who also gave him some elementary knowledge of arithmetic. Cobbett was a brilliant writer, with *Rural Rides*, *Cottage Economy* and the 12 volumes of *The Works of Peter Porcupine* being perhaps his most famous works. In 1800 Cobbett had his own book-shop in Pall Mall, London, and his own publishing house in The Strand. He was also responsible for starting Cobbett's *Political Register* in 1802. He eventually became a Member of Parliament, when he was almost 70 years old. He had always championed the underdog and was known as 'the Poor Man's Friend'. The year before he died he wrote *Cobbett's Legacy to Labourers*. He said it was called a 'Legacy' to remind the working people

> ... that they once had a friend, whom neither love of gain, nor the fear of loss, could seduce from his duty towards God, towards his country, and towards them; will remind them that that friend was born in a cottage and bred to the plough; that men in mighty power were 34 years endeavouring to destroy him; that in spite of this he became a Member of Parliament, freely chosen by the sensible and virtuous and spirited people of Oldham; and that his name was William Cobbett.

Alfred Lord Tennyson (1809-92), Poet Laureate, who lived in the area around Haslemere, was a frequent visitor to Farnham, particularly when he was courting Emily Sellwood (1813-96) from Hale, whom he later married. During her lifetime Lady Emily did not publish anything under her own name although she was, in effect, co-author with her son, Hallam, of *Memoir* (1897). In 1981 Emily's *Journal* was published, being the diary she had compiled from 1850-74 which, together with her *Letters*, published in 1974, has been of great value to scholars of Tennyson.

Black Pond Lane and Wendy's Wood are named from the story of *Peter Pan*, the author of which, Sir James Matthew Barrie (1860-

or to have written about this town, was Izaak Walton (1593-1683), whose *Compleat Angler* contains many worthy passages which have been recorded in books of quotations for decades. Walton stayed at Farnham Castle for a consid-erable time and, bearing in mind the many problems between kings and bishops in those days, his 'I remember that a wise friend of mine did usually say, "that which is every-body's business is nobody's business,"' could well have been an example of the way he lived at the castle—seeing all but saying nothing.

Jonathan Swift (1667-1745) lived at Moor Park, Farnham, and was secretary to Sir William Temple for a number of years. Many tales have been told about a possible relationship between Swift and a young lady called Stella, who lived in a cottage close to Moor Park House, although proof of anything other than a platonic friendship has yet to be found.

1937), lived a mile away from the town centre when he wrote his classic about Peter, Wendy, the Lost Boys and Nana, the St Bernard dog, which has been beloved of children and adults alike for almost a hundred years. Places and names made famous by *Peter Pan* are used by Farnham people for their own addresses in The Bourne and Tilford areas today.

Augustus Toplady, author of the hymn 'Rock of Ages', was born in West Street, and another hymnwriter (for the *Children's Hymn Book*), Mary Anne Sidebotham, lived to the south of the town, where her father was vicar of St Thomas-on-the-Bourne Church.

Other mid-20th century writers of note who found inspiration in this town include Brian Vesey Fitzgerald, who was a national broadcaster and journalist as well as the author of many books about nature and gypsies; H.V. Morton, author of the *In Search Of ...* series, whose son went to St George's School in Castle Street; S.G. Hulme-Beaman, who lived in Rowledge and wrote the famous *Toytown* series of books about Larry the Lamb, a great favourite of the youngsters who listened to *Children's Hour* on the B.B.C. Home Service's radio programme at 5 p.m. each weekday evening; and George Sturt, whose *Change In The Village*, *The Wheelwright's Shop* and *A Small Boy in the Sixties* have all become classics.

Publishers, too, have made their mark in the town with Arthur E. Lucy publishing Surrey's first newspaper, the *Surrey and Hants News*, from 1 The Borough, in 1859, to be followed, in 1892, by Ernest Langham, who founded the *Farnham Herald*, first published in South Street. In more recent years, in the 1960s, Phillimore & Co. Ltd., the publisher of the present book, kept its archives at premises in East Street; *Fishing News* was published from Long Garden Walk in the 1970s and early 1980s; *The American* is printed and published via Farnham Castle Newspapers; Robert Pickens III publishes *TransAtlantic American* from Farnham Maltings; *Revue*, a 'girly' magazine, was once produced at 104a West Street; and Sir Ray Tindle, who owns around 100 newspaper titles, nationwide, has his home and head office in the town.

In the late 1980s, the *Daily Telegraph*'s competition for school newspapers regularly had an entry—*St Christopher's Chronicle*—from the former St Christopher's School, which was also situated in West Street, and the school was proud to receive an award from this national newspaper. At the same time, *The Licensee*, a paper for the licensed trade, was being published from a building adjacent to Farnham Police Station. Charles Hammick, publisher and book-seller, opened his first shop, in Downing Street, Farnham, in 1973.

In the 19th and early 20th centuries many small firms printed and published their own postcards and street directories. In Farnham these were produced by companies such as Sturt and Nichols.

133 Four of the large number of media personalities, who have lived in Farnham, at The Maltings in 1989. Left to right: David Rose, Trevor Macdonald, Desmond Hamill and Alastair Stewart.

Twelve

Frank—the Last and First

134 Frank Cordier, one of the best-known faces in local politics for over forty years. In addition to this work, he and his wife Dorothy ran the Upper Hale Post Office, when it was situated at the junction of Heath Lane and Upper Hale Road. In retirement he lives just a stone's throw away from his former workplace.

THE LAST CHAIRMAN of Waverley Council and the first of Farnham's mayors is Frank Cordier. He has been both a Waverley and Farnham councillor and served on the former Farnham Urban District Council for 26 years. A Justice of the Peace, he was also given the honour of being Chairman of the Court, in May 1987, for his last day as a magistrate after 21 years. It proved to be a day to remember for him, with the remand in custody of three Liverpool men who were accused of conspiracy to rob a Securicor van at Sainsbury's, in South Street, and appearance for the first time of the three men in connection with the *Downing Street Club* murder which had taken place two weeks earlier. Frank, a Londoner, moved to Farnham when he was a small boy. He attended the Bourne School, where the headmaster Andrew Baker was a keen cricketer. In 1936 Frank took seven wickets with seven balls and won two guineas from the *Star* newspaper as a prize.

In its 107-year history the *Farnham Herald* has only had five editors—Ernest Langham, Theo Pope, Oliver Meddows-Taylor, Reg Hatt and Robin Radley. The current position, held by Peter Thompson, is designated editorial manager. When it was first published the *Farnham Herald* was a small paper, hardly larger than A4 format, although today it is a broadsheet. The *Surrey and Hants News*, on the other hand, whose editors have included Arthur E. Lucy, Herbert Penrose, John Penrose and national journalist and author, Guy Bellamy,

135 *Above left*. Ted Parratt, left, and Guy Bellamy, both former national journalists and both former editors of the *Surrey and Hants News*, photographed in the newspaper's former office in West Street. Both are also authors—the former of non-fiction, the latter a well-known novelist whose books have been translated into several languages. Both attended Farnham Grammar School.

136 *Above right*. Frank 'Punch' Parratt, at the top of Burnt Hill in 1928. The area received its name after a fire in 1911, which burned down every tree, according to the late Miriam Vesey-Fitzgerald, who was born that day. 'Punch', a master plasterer, left money at both the *Bat and Ball* and *Hare and Hounds* for his friends to toast him after his death in 1988.

started out in 1859 as a broadsheet but is now a tabloid and is under the umbrella of the *Farnham Herald*. Guy Bellamy was at one time the youngest sub-editor in Fleet Street.

Other Farnham residents employed on national newspapers and magazines include Alan Barter, Diana and Guido Rosignoli, Ted Parratt, Judy Lloyd, Carol Sarler and Gertrude 'Trudie' Pluckrose, a graphic artist with Fleetway Press for 35 years. At 91, she is still drawing and painting in the Abbeyfield House, at Shortheath Crest, where she lives alongside five other women, one of whom is Kathy Blake.

Kathy's father, Lionel, was an undertaker in Shortheath Road (now Farnham Funeral Services). Her great-grandmother, Lucy Clark, who lived next door to the Blake family, was the oldest woman in Wrecclesham in 1902, so she was asked to assist at the tree-planting ceremony, at the top of Sandrock Hill, when an oak was planted to commemorate the coronation of King Edward VII.

Longer lived even than Lucy Clark was the woman known as Granny Morfew, who was born Sarah Parratt in Wrecclesham, in 1786. Granny Morfew was featured in a national magazine called *Titbits*, in 1890, under the heading 'The Oldest Widow in England.' At the time she was 104 and still living alone in a cottage at Ham, near Richmond. A century after Sarah was born, Jonathan Parratt, a relation, held the licence at the *Royal Oak*, Wrecclesham and another Parratt, Esau, held a similar position at the *Bat and Ball* in The Bourne. The Parratt surname is one of the best-known in the Farnham area, together with with those of Othen, Harrington, Pharo, Burningham, Baker and Fry. At one time it was said of Wrecclesham or Rowledge, that every second person a stranger saw was named Parratt. It is also widely believed that it was a person of Parratt descent who picked up William Rufus in the New Forest after he had been shot with an arrow, and

137 John Golley, a former Hurricane and Typhoon pilot, author of many books about the Royal Air Force and personalities such as Sir Frank Whittle, inventor of the jet aircraft engine. His book, *... so few*, published in 1985, was one of the most expensive books ever produced. He was chairman of an advertising firm which he started with the actor, John Slater.

138 Sir John Verney, author, soldier, artist and local politician, who lived at Runwick, is seen here at a Farnham Girls' Grammar School prize-giving ceremony in 1970.

139 The oldest residents in Wrecclesham planted a tree at the road junction of Echo Barn Lane, Sandrock Hill, Shortheath Road and School Hill, in 1902, to commemorate the coronation of King Edward VII. The honour for the women fell to Lucy Clark, in her widow's bonnet, who lived in Shortheath Road, adjacent to Blake's the undertaker (now Farnham Funeral Services).

took the dead king to Winchester in his charcoal cart.

The other Parratt tale concerns King Henry VIII. Most members of the internationally-known P(aeiou)rr(aeiou)tt Society believe that the youngest illegitimate child of this monarch had a Parratt as a mother. Until the Second World War, most members of the Parratt family were involved with hop growing and charcoal burning.

The first art school in Farnham was in The Borough for a short time, until W.H. Allen, its head, moved into a building almost opposite the present-day Liberal Club, in South Street. It was known as Victoria House. In the 1930s the Farnham School of Art, as it was then known, moved to the building at 25 West Street vacated by Farnham Girls' Grammar School pupils who were moving into their purpose-built school in Menin Way. The

140 Art lessons in the open air—in the garden behind the Farnham School of Art. The renowned artist, Otway McCannell, principal there from 1928-45, is standing second right, giving instruction. This photograph was taken for a national magazine but is believed never to have been used. His daughter, Ursula, and grandsons, Tristan, Marcus and Lucien Rees Roberts, are also artists.

141 *Top.* Although the ladies in this 1934/5 photograph look quite mature, they are really children at Hale School taking part in a play, possibly their version of *The Mikado*. The list of surnames of the cast includes many that are typical of the area: Parratt, Slingo, Chadwick, Paine, Varney, Nichols and Knight, plus Guppy, Bushell, Smart, Westmacott, Burden, Barron and Miles.

142 *Above.* Unveiled in 1995 by M.P. Virginia Bottomley and Town Mayor Joan Harris, this plaque in Timber Close/Long Garden Walk reads: 'The greatest timber-framed roof in Europe. The massive, carved frames for the roof of the Great Hall in the Palace of Westminster, were made in Farnham, not far from this spot, and went to London in the summer of 1395.'

number of art students outgrew this building, too, and a new college was constructed in The Hart, to be known as the West Surrey College of Art and Design.

Although in her teens she canvassed on behalf of the Labour Party, helping some of the Jay side of her family, Virginia Bottomley succeeded Maurice Macmillan, a Conservative, who had in turn replaced Sir Godfrey Nicholson, both also Conservatives. Farnham has always returned to Parliament members of this political persuasion.

The Phyllis Tuckwell Hospice, formerly known as Trimmer's Hospital (after the brewery family which paid to have the original hospital built in East Street), is in Menin Way, adjacent to South Farnham School (the old Farnham Girls' Grammar School unit), and cares for dying people from many places besides Farnham.

Farnham Girls' Grammar School, like its counterpart for boys in Morley Road, sent its girls out to all parts of the world and all professions, from Frances Martyr, who became a nun, through to *Sun* Page Three Girl, Jackie Sewell. One of the school caretakers, Mr. W. Avenell, was related to the family of Avenell clockmakers whose timepieces are greatly prized today.

Other watch and clockmakers of the 19th and early 20th century include Borelli, S. and R. Jeffrey and William James in The Borough, Edward James (William's father) and W. Chuter, in Downing Street, W. Hayward, Castle Street, C. Rampton, West Street, and R. Harrington, East Street.

In the 19th century Farnham hops were the most expensive in the country because of their pale green colour and very subtle flavour. They were used in the India Pale Ale which was sent out by the barrel to the military in India. Hops were grown in fields right down to the backs of shops and houses on the town's main streets. Even small children were employed at harvest in picking hops, and these same children trod rushes on the flagstones of the kitchens in their homes, to make ties which could be used by their fathers to hold the hop bines against the strings or poles as they grew. Grain was roasted at Farnham Maltings, hops were dried in the many oast houses in the town and surrounding villages, pockets (sacks) in which the hops were transported, were made in Factory Yard (now Arundell Place), beer was brewed in many kitchens as well as in the breweries in both East and West Street, and was sold in local public

143 The *Coach and Horses*, Castle Street, with licensee J.H. Hewes standing in the doorway. This ex-army officer held the licence here throughout the 1920s and into the '30s. Ale on tap was from the Courage brewery and this company continued to supply the pub for another 60 years. Guy Bellamy's novel, *The Secret Lemonade Drinker*, is set in this hostelry.

144 This line drawing is from a postcard which pre-dates 1911: Charles Smith, saddlers, behind the pub's lamp, moved to South Street at that date. The sign for the *Bell and Crown* dominates the skyline. The carriageway appears to be covered with ironstone setts.

145 A rare photograph of the *Prince of Wales*, Upper Weybourne Lane, Heath End, about seventy years ago, when Mr. G. Lawrence, was the licensee. Despite now being a private house, the new owners have kept as much as possible of the old pub interior. This pub was supplied by Farnham United Breweries with 'all beer drawn from the wood'.

146 The *Jolly Farmer*, Runfold, *c*.1910, almost facing the toll-house on the road to Guildford. In 1931 it was rebuilt to a mock-Tudor design by West Street architects, Harold Falkner and Guy Maxwell Aylwin. This hostelry is now situated on a quiet backwater, following the opening of the Blackwater Valley road in the 1990s.

147 Auction details of a sale which was held at the *Bush Hotel* in 1886. Amongst the public houses which were sold were the *Duke of Cambridge*, East Street (£850), the *White Lion*, Red Lion Lane (£600), the *Lamb*, Abbey Street (£520), the *Alma*, Heath End (£440), the *Green Dragon*, Millbridge, Frensham (£820), the *Cricketers*, Badshot Lea (£1,200), the *Running Stream*, Weybourne (£600) and the *Greyhound*, Hale Road (£830).

SURREY & HANTS

Particulars and Conditions of Sale of

HIGHLY VALUABLE ESTATE,

COMPRISING

THIRTEEN PUBLIC HOUSES,

A PLEASURE FARM,

SEVERAL ENCLOSURES OF WELL CULTIVATED HOP LAND,

LARGE STORES,

SUPERIOR FAMILY RESIDENCES

AND

BUSINESS PREMISES.

Which will be Offered for Sale by Auction, by

MESSRS. NASH & SON AND MR. J. ALFRED EGGAR

[under instructions from the Mortgagees]

AT THE BUSH HOTEL, FARNHAM, SURREY,

On WEDNESDAY, 21st APRIL, 1886,

AT THREE O'CLOCK PRECISELY.

IN TWENTY-ONE LOTS

Particulars and Conditions of Sale may be obtained of
Messrs. HOLLEST, MASON & NASH, Solicitors ;
Messrs. POTTER & CRUNDWELL, Solicitors ;
And of the AUCTIONEERS, (all of) Farnham, Surrey.

148 In the Farnham Town Plan, 1947, Miss Cummins' wool and haberdashery occupies the tall, central building, flanked on either side by Curry's, which sold cycles as well as radios then, and Lipton's, the grocer. On the left can just be seen Flinn's, the dry cleaners. On the right is the London Central Meat Company. Only Curry's remains but has moved from 119 to 118, West Street.

houses, many of which were scarcely more than the front parlour of a house and only held beer licences rather than full wine, spirit and beer permits. It is widely believed that at the height of the 19th-century beer trade, Farnham had more pubs per head of population than any other town in the country; Frank Cordier, mentioned earlier, also knew a great deal about hostelries, his stepfather, Mr. F. Foot having held the licence at the *Lion and Lamb Tap*.

Farnham is a place where people have chosen to live for 8,000 years and it is impossible to do more than to scratch the surface, with one of the mesolithic flint tools, in a volume such as this. It would be difficult, in one person's lifetime, to find out all there is to know about this town but I hope that *Farnham Past* has been able to whet your appetite to delve further into the secrets which it still holds.

Bibliography

Ewbank Smith, B., *Farnham in War and Peace* (1983)

Ewbank Smith, B., *Edwardian Farnham* (1979)

Ewbank Smith, B., *Victorian Farnham* (1971)

Farnham Chamber of Commerce, *The Book of Farnham in Surrey* (1925)

Hack, R.E., *Entanglements* (1994)

Hall, D.E. and Gretton, F., *Farnham During the Civil Wars and Interregnum 1642-1660* (1982)

Harper, Daphne, *The Cost of Living in 1300* (1964)

Hewins, Maurice, *Between Four Bridges* (1977)

Homeland Handbook: *Farnham with its surroundings* (1914)

Leman Hare, T., *The Portrait Book of our Kings and Queens 1066-1911* (1911)

Lynn, Vera, *Vocal Refrain* (1975)

Manning, Elfrida, *Saxon Farnham* (1970)

Morris, John (ed.), *Domesday Book: Surrey* (1975)

Newnam, W.E., *The Story of Farnham* (1969)

Nichols, John, *Directory* (1872)

Pigot and Co., *Farnham in 1839* (1839)

Robo, Etienne, *Medieval Farnham* (1935)

Spring, Lawrence & Hall, Derek, *The Farnham Greencoats* (1987)

Sturt, George, *Change in the Village* (1912)

Sturt, George, *The Wheelwright's Shop* (1923)

Temple, N., *Farnham Buildings and People*, 2nd edn. (1973)

Wade, A.G., *Farnham Castle*, 3rd edn. (1956)

Ware, Gwen, *The White Monks of Waverley* (1976)

Burrow's Pocket Guides: *The 'Borough' Guide to Farnham* (1920)

Mate's Guide (1903)

Newsletters of the Farnham and District Museum Society

The Story of a School F.G.G.S. 1901-1973 (1973)

A History of Farnham Grammar School in Surrey (1991)

Index

Figures in **bold** type are the page numbers of illustrations in the text

A. BUCK,

"Surrey Arms," East Street, Farnham

WINE & SPIRIT MERCHANT.

HORSES & TRAPS;
PRIVATE OMNIBU
To let on Hire at shortest notice.

CANUTE & Co.,
ERSHOT, FARNHAM and FLEE

THE BOOT STORE,
44, BOROUGH, FARNHAM

HOLDEN BROTHE
Invite inspection of their New Stock of
* BOOTS & SHOES.

GENTLEMEN'S BOOTS,
10/6 TO 25/-

DRESS
SHOES.

WATERPROOF "K" BOOTS.
GENTLEMEN'S
WALKING
Shoes

HALF GUINEA BOOTS.

LADIES'
WALKING
BOOTS.
BUTTON
AND LACE
SHOES.

To A. E
CARPENTER, * JOINER * A
ESTIMATES GIVEN FOR G
PAINTER.

Mrs. Wilson,
The Gift Shop

To F. STURT
Booksel Bookbinders
BUI
Millwrigh

WHERE TO SHOP AT FARNHAM.
W. R. WORSAM,
BAKER, PASTRY COOK
AND CONFECTIONER,
24 & 25 DOWNING STREET, FARNHAM
Established over a Century.
ICES, CREAMS, AND JELLIES.
BRIDE, CHRISTENING, BIRTHDAY, AND
SCHOOL CAKES MADE TO ORDER.
DANCES AN TIONS CATERED FOR.
Refreshment Roo

48,

ription

W. AYLING,

Agent for Triumphs, Hu
and
— REPAIRS

Meat Supplied fed o
al Farms, and
st Quality only.

... K. WORSAM L
Bakers, Pastrycooks and Confectioners
24 & 25 DOWNING STREET · FAR

C. GRINST
Family Butc
ROWLEDGE
Su
FAMILIE